Critical Reasoning

Custom Edition for UC-Davis, Professor Gilmore

Jerry Cederblom | David Paulsen

CENGAGE
Learning™

Australia • Brazil • Japan • Korea • Mexico • Singapore • Spain • United Kingdom • United States

Critical Reasoning: Custom Edition for UC-Davis, Professor Gilmore

Jerry Cederblom | David Paulsen

Executive Editors:
Michele Baird
Maureen Staudt
Michael Stranz

Project Development Manager:
Linda deStefano

Senior Marketing Coordinators:
Sara Mercurio
Lindsay Shapiro

Senior Production / Manufacturing Manager:
Donna M. Brown

PreMedia Services Supervisor:
Rebecca A. Walker

Rights & Permissions Specialist:
Kalina Hintz

Cover Image:
Getty Images*

* Unless otherwise noted, all cover images used by Custom Solutions, a part of Cengage Learning, have been supplied courtesy of Getty Images with the exception of the Earthview cover image, which has been supplied by the National Aeronautics and Space Administration (NASA).

For product information and technology assistance, contact us at
Cengage Learning Customer & Sales Support, 1-800-354-9706

For permission to use material from this text or product, submit all requests online at **cengage.com/permissions**
Further permissions questions can be emailed to
permissionrequest@cengage.com

ISBN-13: **978-1-111-29634-6**

ISBN-10: **1-111-29634-0**

Cengage Learning
5191 Natorp Boulevard
Mason, Ohio 45040
USA

Cengage Learning is a leading provider of customized learning solutions with office locations around the globe, including Singapore, the United Kingdom, Australia, Mexico, Brazil, and Japan. Locate your local office at:
international.cengage.com/region

Cengage Learning products are represented in Canada by Nelson Education, Ltd.

For your lifelong learning solutions, visit **custom.cengage.com**

Visit our corporate website at **cengage.com**

Cengage Learning purchased [enter business unit name] from Thomson on July 5, 2007

Printed in the United States of America

Custom Table of Contents

Critical Reasoning, 6th Edition, Jerry Cederblom | David Paulsen

 CHAPTER TWO

The Anatomy of Arguments: Identifying Premises and Conclusions

When someone gives reasons to support a point of view, that person is usually offering an *argument*. You encounter arguments in your reading and in your conversations with others, and you commonly offer arguments to support your own beliefs. When you are presented with an argument, you can take the opportunity to decide whether the reasons given are good enough to warrant incorporating the point of view that is being advanced into your own set of beliefs. To make this decision, you need to clearly understand the argument and then evaluate it.

The main focus of this and several of the following chapters is a kind of argument called *deductive*. But before we begin our study of deductive arguments, we should provide a broader view of arguments, including nondeductive arguments. Since an argument gives reasons (one or more) in support of a point of view, both of the following examples would surely count as arguments. In each of them, at least one reason is given to support a point of view.

Example 2.1	**Deductive Argument** *Eliminating plea bargaining would overwhelm the court system with criminal trials. If it would do this, then plea bargaining should not be eliminated. Therefore, plea bargaining should not be eliminated.*
Example 2.2	**Informally Stated Argument** *Any practice that could help cure disease while not causing harm should be continued. So using embryonic stem cells in research should be continued.*

Although these examples give reason(s) in support of a viewpoint, important differences exist between them. Example 2.1 has a form or structure that makes the conclusion follow necessarily from the premises. That is, if the premises are true, then the conclusion must be true. It's an example of a *deductive argument*.

If an argument doesn't already have a structure that makes the conclusion follow from the premises, we could try to restate it so that it does have such a structure. For example, we could treat Example 2.2 as being a fragment of a longer, more complete, deductive argument.

Example 2.2
Restated as a
Complete
Deductive
Argument

Any practice that could help cure diseases while not causing harm should be continued. **Using embryonic stem cells in research could help cure diseases while not causing harm.** *So using embryonic stem cells in research should be continued.*

When we add the middle (boldfaced) sentence to Example 2.2, we are restating it in a way that makes the conclusion—*using embryonic stem cells in research should be continued*—follow necessarily from the premises. Some might claim that the middle sentence is already *implicit* in the original example. If this is taken to mean that anyone who asserts the original argument must have "had in mind" the unstated premise, *using embryonic stem cells in research could help cure diseases while not causing harm,* then we are not committed to this view. We aren't guessing what the arguer had in mind. Rather, when we add this premise to create a complete deductive argument, we are trying to make it easier to decide whether to accept the argument's conclusion. By adding the unstated premise, we can see all of the statements we would have to judge as acceptable or unacceptable in order to decide whether this argument compels us to accept its conclusion. The premises of a deductive argument are like a checklist: Is it reasonable to believe that any practice that could help cure diseases while not causing harm should be continued? Is it reasonable to believe that using fetal cells in research could cure diseases while not causing harm? If there are no reasonable grounds for rejecting either of these claims, then I am driven to the conclusion that using embryonic stem cells in research should be continued.

For the next several chapters, our general approach will be to interpret arguments as deductive. If they are not stated as complete deductive arguments, we will try to restate them so that they are. Later chapters will study certain kinds of arguments that, for purposes of evaluation, might be best interpreted as nondeductive. If an argument is *nondeductive,* its conclusion doesn't necessarily follow from its premises. If the argument is successful, its premises provide *some support* for the conclusion; but even if the premises are true, the conclusion could be false.

Examples 2.3, 2.4, and 2.5 could all be taken as nondeductive. Example 2.3 gives three reasons against legalizing physician-assisted suicide. These reasons could be presented as having *some weight,* even if it doesn't follow necessarily that physician-assisted suicide should be illegal. The argument might be taken as

Some Types of Nondeductive Arguments

Example 2.3

Convergent Argument

Legalizing physician-assisted suicide would lead to (1) helping disabled people die who are not terminally ill, (2) helping people die who are depressed and might later want to live, and (3) helping people die in order merely to save medical expense. These are all reasons against legalizing physician-assisted suicide.

Example 2.4

Inductive Argument

The rate of violent crime fell last year in a sample of fifty U.S. cities and towns, so it is likely that the rate fell in the nation as a whole.

Example 2.5

Argument from Analogy

The universe has an order and precision similar to a clock's. Since the clock had a maker, the universe probably had a maker.

leaving open the possibility that considerations in favor of legalization outweigh considerations against it.

Of course, Example 2.3 could also be interpreted as a deductive argument that is not completely stated. It could be taken as having the implicit premise that if legalizing physician-assisted suicide would have these three results, then it should be kept illegal. The conclusion that physician-assisted suicide should be kept illegal would then follow necessarily. In the next several chapters, we will interpret arguments such as Example 2.3 as deductive, but in chapter 9 we will introduce an alternative way of viewing them: that is, as a kind of nondeductive argument sometimes called *convergent*.

Example 2.4 is typical of a kind of argument called *inductive*. Its premise describes a characteristic found in a sample (fifty U.S. cities and towns). The conclusion asserts that *likely* this same characteristic—a decline in the rate of violent crime—is true of a larger population (the nation as a whole). The fact that this conclusion asserts only a probability is what makes this kind of argument nondeductive. Example 2.5 is called an *argument from analogy*. It argues that two things are alike in certain respects, so they are probably alike in some further respect. As with the previous example, the conclusion—the universe had a maker—is asserted as probable only, not as necessarily following from the premise, so this, too, is best interpreted as a *nondeductive* argument.

All five examples, then, constitute *arguments* in the broad sense that they give one or more reasons in support of a point of view. The reasons are called *premises,* and the point of view being supported is called the *conclusion*. Chapters 8 and 9 will provide techniques for understanding and evaluating nondeductive arguments.

We now turn to the task of identifying premises and conclusions of deductive arguments.

The Key to Identification: Seeing What Is Supported by What

To understand deductive arguments fully, you first need to learn to identify their parts—the **premises** and the **conclusion.** This will ultimately help you to evaluate arguments better. As in medicine, you must learn the anatomy of an animal before you can systematically diagnose its ills and improve its health.

We will begin our investigation of premises and conclusions by looking at short, simplified passages that contain arguments. For example, a reader of the editorial on smoking reprinted later in this chapter might restate one of its arguments in this way:

Example 2.6   *If smoking poses a risk to the health of bystanders, then it violates their rights. Smoking does pose a risk to the health of bystanders. Therefore, smoking violates the rights of bystanders.*

The first two statements support the third. They provide reasons for believing that smoking violates the rights of bystanders, so each one individually is a premise of the argument. The conclusion is the statement that the premises are supposed to support: Smoking violates the rights of bystanders.

Consider a second example. Suppose someone who doesn't know much about biology argues as follows:

Example 2.7   *Whales are not mammals, since no fish are mammals, and whales are fish.*

In this argument the premises and the conclusion are not given in separate sentences, but we can nevertheless distinguish what is supported from what is offered as support. The first clause, *whales are not mammals,* is supposed to be supported by the two clauses that follow: *no fish are mammals* and *whales are fish.* The latter two statements are the premises, and the first statement, whales are not mammals, is the conclusion. This conclusion happens to be false, but it is nevertheless the conclusion of the argument—a faulty argument in this case.

Two cautions are in order: (1) Some people misconstrue the conclusion as a mere summary of the premises. The conclusion of an argument does not, however, simply restate the sentences in a passage. (2) Others tend to think of the conclusion as the most important point in the passage. Often it is, but it need not be. The conclusion can be singled out because it stands in a special relationship to the other statements—that is, it is supposed to be supported by the other statements. To find the conclusion in a passage, we must see which statement is supposed to be supported by the others.

Clues to Identifying Argument Parts: Indicator Words

Sometimes the person offering an argument provides clues that identify the premises and conclusion. Consider the following pessimistic argument about gun control:

Example 2.8   *Either we ban all handguns or homicide rates will remain high. We will not ban all handguns. We can conclude that homicide rates will remain high.*

In this case the speaker tells us which statement is the conclusion of the argument by using the phrase "We can conclude that." We call expressions that serve this purpose *conclusion indicators*. Numerous expressions can play this role, including the following:

CONCLUSION INDICATORS

  so

  thus

  therefore

  hence

  we can conclude that

  consequently

There are also expressions that help identify premises. Among the most common of these are:

PREMISE INDICATORS[1]

  since

  for

  because

  for the reason that

The statement that immediately follows a conclusion indicator is the conclusion; that following a premise indicator is a premise. This latter will seem natural when you consider that premises are reasons given in support of the conclusion, and all the premise indicators mean roughly "for the reason that."

---

1. These words are not always used as premise indicators. For example, *since* can also be used to indicate order in time, as in the statement, "Since (that is, *in the time since*) Joe went to medical school, he has established a practice in the field of AIDS treatment."

Additional indicators typically come between premises and conclusions:

PREMISE AND CONCLUSION INDICATORS		
(premise)	. . . shows that . . .	(conclusion)
"	. . . indicates that . . .	"
"	. . . proves that . . .	"
"	. . . entails that . . .	"
"	. . . implies that . . .	"
"	. . . establishes that . . .	"
"	. . . allows us to infer that . . .	"
"	. . . gives us reasons for believing that . . .	"

Or, alternatively, they come between conclusions and premises:

CONCLUSION AND PREMISE INDICATORS		
(conclusion)	. . . is shown by . . .	(premise)
"	. . . is indicated by . . .	"
"	. . . is proven by . . .	"
"	. . . is entailed by . . .	"
"	. . . is implied by . . .	"
"	. . . is established by . . .	"

Marking the Parts of Arguments

The distinction between the premises and conclusion in an argument can be marked more formally in several ways. We can graphically set them apart by putting the argument into a *standard form*. To do this, we list the premises, numbering each separate statement. Then we draw a line to separate premises from the conclusion. The conclusion is below the line. Traditionally, conclusions have been marked by a sign consisting of three dots. The argument in Example 2.8 would be written in standard form as

Example 2.8 in Standard Form

(1) Either we ban all handguns or homicide rates will remain high.

(2) We will not ban all handguns.

∴ *Homicide rates will remain high.*

Note that we leave out premise and conclusion indicators, as well as words that connect the premises, such as *and* or *but*.[2] These words become unnecessary because

---

2. If the word *and* occurs within a premise rather than between premises, it should not be omitted.

our manner of displaying the argument already indicates which statements are premises, how many there are, and what is asserted as the conclusion.

For simple arguments written out in detail, a second, abbreviated version of the process of putting an argument in standard form is to circle the parts of a passage that contain premises and the conclusion and mark the premises with the symbols Pr_1, Pr_2, and so on, and the conclusion with C. Take a look at Example 2.9.

Example 2.9

Pr_1

(Since whales and dolphins are mammals) and

(mammals need to breathe air,) Pr_2

(whales and dolphins need to breathe air.) C

Notice that premises and the conclusion must be complete statements. In Example 2.10, the fragment "If smoking poses a risk to the health of bystanders" alone can't serve as a premise because it is not a complete statement. Notice as well that this argument contains three premises as well as the conclusion.

Example 2.10

Pr_1 (If smoking poses a risk to the health of bystanders, then it violates their rights.)

Pr_2 (If smoking violates the rights of bystanders, smoking in public ought to be restricted.) (Smoking does pose a risk to the health of bystanders.) Therefore,

C (smoking in public ought to be restricted.) Pr_3

Theoretically, there is no limit to the number of premises an argument can contain. However, most arguments found in ordinary discourse contain only a few premises.

Exercise 2.1   **Techniques for Marking the Parts of Arguments**

Try these techniques in the following exercises. Put exercises 1 and 2 into *standard form;* for exercises 3–16, *circle and label* the premises and conclusions.

1. Any friend of mine deserves my respect. Ed is a friend of mine. Therefore, Ed deserves my respect.

(In standard form:)

(1) _____

(2) _____

∴

2. Abortion raises serious moral questions because abortion involves the taking of a human life, and anything that involves the taking of a human life raises serious moral questions.

(In standard form:)

(1)

(2)

∴

(Circle and label the premises and conclusion in the following exercises.)

3. If your mind were organized, your desk would be organized. Your desk isn't organized. It follows that your mind isn't organized.

4. If a child has formed a strong bond with the family that adopted her, then the biological parents should not reclaim her. Natalie has formed a strong bond with the family that adopted her. Hence, her biological parents should not reclaim her.

5. An activity pays if the people who engage in it come out ahead economically more often than not. The people who engage in many crimes come out ahead economically more often than not. It follows that many crimes pay.

6. The computer will alter society in many unpredictable ways for the reason that all major technological advances alter society in many unpredictable ways, and the computer is a major technological advance.

7. It is wrong for society to kill a murderer. This follows for the reason that if a murderer is wrong in killing his victim, then society is also wrong in killing the murderer. And a murderer is wrong in killing his victim.

8. All pornography should be banned. This allows us to infer that *National Geographic* magazine should be banned, because anything that contains pictures of naked adults and children is pornographic, and *National Geographic* contains pictures of naked adults and children.

9. If private enterprise does better than government at running businesses, then it will do better at running schools. Private enterprise does better at running businesses. We can conclude that private enterprise will do better at running schools.

10. Any area of study that contributes to the field of medicine should be well supported. Therefore, biology should be well supported, since it contributes to the field of medicine.

11. If privatizing schools would leave poorer, more-difficult-to-educate students at a disadvantage, then privatizing schools will only worsen the problems of

inner cities. It follows that privatizing schools will worsen the problems of inner cities since privatizing would leave poorer, more-difficult-to-educate students at a disadvantage.

12. If you have an irresponsible mate, then either you should avoid having a child or you should prepare yourself for the difficulties of single parenting. Hence, you should avoid having a child since you do have an irresponsible mate, and you don't want to prepare yourself for the difficulties of single parenting.

It might seem more difficult to identify premises and conclusions in passages with long, complex sentences. Actually, the task remains fairly simple if you can locate the indicator words that divide an argument into its parts, as in the following exercises.

13. Capital punishment should be abolished. This is so because a nonwhite murderer whose victim is white is much more likely to be executed than a white murderer whose victim is either white or nonwhite. If that is the case, then either this kind of discrimination should be eliminated, or the death penalty should be abolished. Unfortunately, this kind of discrimination cannot be eliminated.

14. If capital punishment deters potential murderers, then if it is not inflicted, some innocent person will be murdered. It is better for a murderer to be executed than for an innocent person to be murdered. Thus, if capital punishment deters potential murderers, then it should be inflicted.

15. Since smoking is addictive, we can conclude that production of cigarettes should be more tightly restricted. This is because if smoking is addictive, then cigarette companies are trafficking in addictive substances; and if cigarette companies are trafficking in addictive substances, production of cigarettes should be more tightly restricted.

16. If Americans reject congressional candidates who propose to rein in spending on medicare and farm subsidies, then either we will suffer from a growing deficit or we will need to raise taxes. The public won't tolerate raising taxes, and Americans will reject candidates who propose to rein in spending on medicare and farm subsidies. It follows that we will suffer from a growing deficit.

What to Do When There Are No Indicator Words: The Principle of Charitable Interpretation

Indicator words explicitly mark the intended role of statements in an argument. But authors often omit indicator words on the assumption that it is obvious which of their statements are offered as support and which statement is being supported. When there are no indicator words, and it is questionable what an argument's premises or conclusion are, you should employ what might be called the *Principle of Charitable Interpretation:*

> **Principle of Charitable Interpretation:** When more than one interpretation of an argument is possible, the argument should be interpreted so that the premises provide the strongest support for the conclusion.

This principle is in keeping with the rationale for critical reasoning offered in chapter 1. The object is not to make your opponent's argument look as weak as possible but to decide what is most reasonable to believe. It is to this end that arguments under consideration should be given the strongest possible interpretation.

One way to identify the premises and conclusion is to try each statement of an argument in the role of conclusion, with the remaining statements acting as premises. Whichever statement is best supported by the others should be taken to be the conclusion. Note the following argument:

Example 2.11   *You should have come to the meeting. You promised Alicia you would come. If you promise to do something, you should do it.*

It can be seen fairly readily that the first statement is better supported by the remainder of the argument than either of the other two. If we put the argument into standard form, alternating each statement in the role of conclusion, we can see more easily that this reading is the best. Although this lengthy process is seldom necessary in actually interpreting an argument, it might be helpful in this case to go through it to show how the plausibility of the different alternatives varies.

Putting the argument into standard form with the first sentence as the conclusion gives us

Reading 1   *(1) If you promise to do something, you should do it.*

(2) You promised Alicia you would come.

∴ *You should have come to the meeting.*

This interpretation of the passage is best because if the premises are true, the conclusion must also be true. And, as will be explained in succeeding chapters, this is precisely the relationship of support between premises and conclusion that is one requirement for a good deductive argument. By considering what each statement means, you can see that the premises adequately support the conclusion. The first premise states that if you satisfy a certain condition (making a promise), then you have an obligation (keeping the promise). The second premise adds that you did satisfy the condition of promising something (that is, to come to the meeting). If these premises are true, then the conclusion—*you should have come to the meeting*—must be true.

In contrast, the supposed premises in the other readings do not adequately support their supposed conclusions. The premises could be true without the conclusion being true.

Reading 2   *(1) You should have come to the meeting.*

(2) You promised Alicia you would come.

∴ *If you promise to do something, you should do it.*

It could be true that you should have come to the meeting, and that you promised Alicia, but these facts do nothing to support the more general conclusion that if you promise to do something, you should do it.

Reading 3   *(1) You should have come to the meeting.*

(2) If you promise to do something, you should do it.

∴ *You promised Alicia you would come.*

The claims that you should have come, and that if you promise something, you should do it, do not support the claim that you promised Alicia you would come. It could be that you should have come (you would have had the chance to meet some interesting people), and that you should keep your promises; but it could at the same time be false that you promised Alicia you would come.

Again, in actual practice, the context in which you find a passage limits the number of possible interpretations that can reasonably be made. The formulation of the Principle of Charitable Interpretation given here should be taken as preliminary and subject to this qualification.

Exercise 2.2   **Using the Principle of Charitable Interpretation to Pick Out Premises and Conclusions in Arguments Without Explicit Indicator Words**

Identify the premises and the conclusion in each of the following arguments. Interpret each argument so that the premises give the best support for the conclusion. As we have indicated, arguments do not ordinarily occur in such simplified form, with every statement in a passage serving as either a premise or a conclusion. We are presenting these stylized passages to sharpen your skills at identifying argument parts.

1. If you buy a fur coat, then you are supporting the fur industry. If you are supporting the fur industry, then you are encouraging cruel treatment of

animals. If you buy a fur coat, you are encouraging cruel treatment of animals.

2. Either the government should protect children from abuse and neglect by their parents, or it should reinstitute orphanages. The government will not protect children from abuse and neglect by their parents. The government should reinstitute orphanages.

3. Every person should avoid keeping loaded guns around the house. All those who have the capacity to kill should avoid keeping loaded guns around the house. Every person has the capacity to kill.

4. You will dread growing older. If you take too much pride in your physical appearance, you will dread growing older. You take too much pride in your physical appearance.

5. Anyone who is overly ambitious will alienate her friends. Sheila is overly ambitious. Sheila will alienate her friends.

6. If you respected my opinion, you would seek my advice. You don't seek my advice. You don't respect my opinion.

7. Either the United States will tackle the real social ills that beset its cities or it will lose the "war on drugs." The United States will not tackle the real social ills that beset its cities. The United States will lose the "war on drugs."

8. All restrictions on smoking are restrictions on personal freedom. All restrictions on personal freedom are in need of strong justification. All restrictions on smoking are in need of strong justification.

9. Any gun law gives advantage to lawbreakers. Anything that gives an advantage to lawbreakers makes law-abiders less safe. Any gun law makes law-abiders less safe.

10. The ban on selling hypodermic needles should be lifted. If we want to combat AIDS, then we must prevent drug users from sharing dirty needles. If we must prevent the sharing of dirty needles, then the ban on selling needles should be lifted. And obviously, we do want to combat AIDS.

11. If capital punishment deterred murder better than life imprisonment, then states with capital punishment would have lower murder rates than comparable states with life imprisonment only. States with capital punishment do not have lower murder rates than comparable states with life imprisonment only. Capital punishment does not deter murder better than life imprisonment.

12. Couples should be discouraged from marrying young. Marriage takes a great adjustment. If it takes a great adjustment and the young find such adjustment difficult, they should be discouraged from marrying. The young find adjustment to the demands of marriage difficult.

Patterns of Argument

The Principle of Charitable Interpretation asks us to interpret an argument so that the statements we take as premises best support the statement we take as the conclusion.[3] We have assumed that you are already able to see, in the simplest cases, which statement is best supported by the remaining statements. But to become clearer about this relationship of support, consider two ways of interpreting the following argument:

Argument   *If my car is out of fuel, it won't start. My car won't start. My car is out of fuel.*

Interpretation 1

(1) *If my car is out of fuel, it won't start.*

(2) *My car is out of fuel.*

∴ *My car won't start.*

Interpretation 2

(1) *If my car is out of fuel, it won't start.*

(2) *My car won't start.*

∴ *My car is out of fuel.*

In interpretation 2, the conclusion does not follow from the premises. There are other reasons a car might not start than that it is out of fuel; perhaps the ignition system has failed. Even if the first premise is true and the car does not start, it doesn't follow that it is without fuel. Now contrast this to interpretation 1. If it is true that the absence of fuel prevents starting, then it is unavoidable that if you are out of fuel, the car will not start. We can't find a situation for interpretation 1 (like the ignition problem for interpretation 2) that would make the premises true but the conclusion false.

You could try to reason through to the best interpretation in this way each time you encounter a passage without indicator words and are unsure of what to pick as premises and what as the conclusion. But it is helpful to note that the two interpretations that were just considered are instances of argument patterns that you will encounter again and again; every time you see an instance of the pattern in interpretation 1, the conclusion does follow from the premises, whereas for the pattern in interpretation 2, the conclusion doesn't follow.

A pattern involves the repetition of elements. In interpretation 1, the two statements are repeated: *My car is out of fuel* and *It (my car) won't start.* It is customary to

---

3. Again, when you apply this principle, you are limited by what can plausibly be interpreted as the intent of the passage.

represent these elements by letters.[4] The pattern in interpretation 1 might be represented as:

(1) If A, then B.

(2) A.

∴ *B.*

         MODUS PONENS or
AFFIRMING THE ANTECEDENT

This pattern is so common that it has been given a name: *modus ponens.*[5] The faulty pattern in interpretation 2 might be represented as:

(1) If A, then B.

(2) B.

∴ *A.*

       AFFIRMING THE CONSEQUENT
(Faulty)

Even though this is a faulty pattern, it is common enough that it also has acquired a name. It is known as the *fallacy of affirming the consequent* (because the second premise *affirms* the "then . . ." part,—that is, the *consequent* of the first premise).

    The point of the foregoing discussion is that if a passage could be fit into either of the two patterns, the Principle of Charitable Interpretation would dictate fitting into the *modus ponens* pattern, because with this interpretation the premises provide the best support for the conclusion.

    A related but different pair of interpretations can be given for the argument: If you respected my opinion, you would seek my advice. You don't seek my advice. You don't respect my opinion. Here are two ways of identifying the premises and conclusion:

Interpretation 1
    (1) If you respected my opinion, you would seek my advice.

    (2) You don't seek my advice.

    ∴ *You don't respect my opinion.*

---

4. In the example we use the letters *A* and *B*, but you could use other letters—for example, *F*—to remind us of the statement involving *Fuel* and *S* to remind us of a statement containing *Start*.

5. Notice that what remains after the repeated elements are marked by the letters *A* and *B* is the expression "if . . . then." This expression along with "or" and "and" are called *logical connectives*—they connect two statements. Special symbols are sometimes used to represent them: the arrow, →, for "if . . . then"; the ampersand, &, for ". . . and . . ."; the *vel,* ∨, for "or." This way of showing form is discussed at greater length in chapter 5, which covers a more formal approach to deductive arguments. We could represent *modus ponens* as:

    (1) A → B.

    (2) A.

    ∴ *B.*

Interpretation 2   *(1) If you respected my opinion, you would seek my advice.*

(2) You don't respect my opinion.

∴ *You don't seek my advice.*

In interpretation 1, the conclusion does follow from the premises. The first premise states that *if you respected my opinion, then you would seek my advice.* Suppose, as the second premise states, you don't seek my advice. Now in order to make both these premises true, we are compelled to say that you don't respect my opinion. If we tried to claim both that the first premise is true and that you do respect my opinion, then we would be forced to say that you would seek my advice. But this would make the second premise false. In other words, the only possible way to make both premises true is to make the conclusion true also. This pattern of argument is called *modus tollens* and is represented as:[6]

(1) If A, then B.

(2) Not B.

∴ *Not A.*

MODUS TOLLENS or DENYING THE CONSEQUENT

In interpretation 2, the conclusion *doesn't follow from the premises.* It very well could be that if you did respect my opinion, you would seek my advice. (Suppose you need information badly and will go to any source you consider reliable.) It also could be that you don't respect my opinion; maybe you have heard that I have been mistaken more times than not. But it doesn't follow that you won't seek my advice. You might do so just to flatter me and keep me as a friend. That is, there might be more than one reason for a given consequent. It is perfectly possible for the premises of this argument to be true without the conclusion being true.

Arguments of this pattern are often persuasive, even though they shouldn't be. The pattern, called *denying the antecedent,* looks like this:

(1) If A, then B.

(2) Not A.

∴ *Not B.*

DENYING THE ANTECEDENT
(Faulty)

Although there are numerous argument patterns besides *modus ponens* and *modus tollens* whose premises guarantee the truth of their conclusions, there are a few that occur so frequently that they are worth learning at the outset. The following

---

6. In addition to the symbols →, &, and ∨ for "if . . . then," "and," and "or," the symbol ¬ or just a dash, −, is often used for "It is not the case that. . . ." Unlike the first three symbols, which come between two statements, ¬ stands in front of a single sentence. Using this symbol, we can represent *modus tollens* in this way: *(1) A → B.*
(2) ¬ B.

∴ *¬ A.*

chart displays seven common argument patterns, including *modus ponens* and *modus tollens*. Any argument that fits one of these patterns will satisfy the criterion that if the premises are true, the conclusion must be true. Therefore, any plausible reading of a passage that fits one of these patterns would be supported by the Principle of Charitable Interpretation.

Some Common Successful Argument Patterns

Statement-Based Patterns	Argument Pattern	Examples
	i. Modus Ponens	
	(1) If A, then B.	*(1) If I lie, then I'll be sorry.*
	(2) A.	*(2) I'll lie.*
	∴ B.	*∴ I'll be sorry.*
	ii. Disjunctive Argument	
	(1) Either A or B.	*(1) Either I should exercise or I should diet.*
	(2) Not A.	*(2) I should not exercise.*
	∴ B.	*∴ I should diet.*
	iii. Modus Tollens	
	(1) If A, then B.	*(1) If you study, then you learn.*
	(2) Not B.	*(2) You didn't learn.*
	∴ Not A.	*∴ You didn't study.*
	iv. Hypothetical Argument	
	(1) If A, then B.	*(1) If I pay now, then I'll save.*
	(2) If B, then C.	*(2) If I'll save, then I'll have money later.*
	∴ If A, then C.	*∴ If I pay now, then I'll have money later.*
	v. Chain Argument	
	(1) A.	*(1) The whole group is coming.*
	(2) If A, then B.	*(2) If the whole group is coming, then we'll need more refreshments.*
	(3) If B, then C.	*(3) If we'll need more refreshments, then we'll have to go to the store again.*
	∴ C.	*∴ We'll have to go to the store again.*

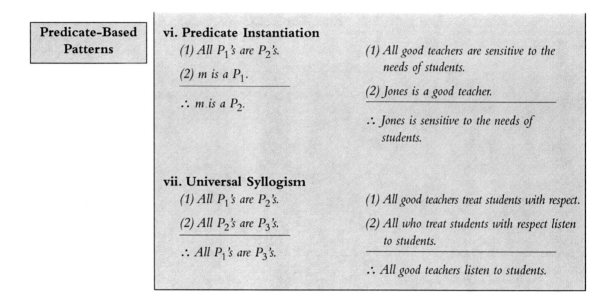

The capital letters *A*, *B*, and *C* in patterns i–v stand for whole *statements;* we call this type of argument pattern *statement-based.* In patterns vi and vii, the terms P_1, P_2, and P_3 stand for parts of statements, such as "good teacher," which refer to classes of objects. The lowercase letter *m* in pattern vi stands for a name or description of a particular person or thing. These names or descriptions can be seen as subjects that fit with a *predicate* such as "is a good teacher" to form a whole statement: "Jones is a good teacher." We will call the argument patterns vi and vii *predicate-based.* This chart provides only a sample of commonly found successful patterns. We discuss what makes them "successful" and how to determine whether a prospective pattern represents a *valid deductive* argument form in chapter 4.

By becoming familiar with these patterns, you will get a feel for the kind of relationship between premises and conclusions you are looking for when you apply the Principle of Charitable Interpretation. Chapters 4 and 5 discuss argument patterns in greater detail, explaining some of the ways to determine whether an argument pattern is successful.

Exercise 2.3

Using Argument Patterns to Pick Out Premises and Conclusions in Arguments Without Explicit Indicator Words

---

Each of the exercises in this section fits one of the patterns identified on the preceding pages or a combination of them. Several tips will help you to identify these patterns in written arguments. First, the order of the premises makes no difference:

(1) If B, then C.

(2) A.

(3) If A, then B.

∴ C.

exhibits the same pattern for our purposes as

(1) A.

(2) If A, then B.

(3) If B, then C.

∴ C.

Second, in an either-or type sentence, order does not make any difference (though it does in an if-then type sentence):

(1) Either B or A.

(2) Not A.

∴ B.

exhibits the same pattern as

(1) Either A or B.

(2) Not A.

∴ B.

Third, arguments can fit these patterns even if some key words are missing. For example, if-then sentences often occur without the *then,* as in: "If you lend me ten dollars, I'll love you forever." They may even have the *if* part at the end of the sentence, as in: "I'll bring the food, if you'll bring the wine." Either-or type sentences may occur without the *either* stated: "I'll have coffee or tea." And the word *all* may be replaced by other expressions such as *every* or *any,* as in: "Every person needs a friend."

In the process of identifying premises and a conclusion, other features of a passage may provide further clues. First, since the conclusion is often the main point in an argumentative passage, look carefully at readings that treat the beginning or the final sentences as the conclusion. Second, the conclusion of an argument is seldom longer and more complex than the premises. For example, we should be suspicious of a reading in which the conclusion is an if-then sentence but the premises are not.

As we have indicated, arguments do not ordinarily occur in such simplified form. We are presenting these "unnatural" passages to sharpen your skill at identifying premises, conclusions, and argument patterns.

1. Go back to Exercise 2.2 and use the argument patterns to identify premises and conclusions. Note any arguments you interpreted incorrectly before you learned the argument patterns.

2. Identify the premises and conclusion, as well as the argument pattern, for each of the following exercises:

   a. John is bound to sharpen his argumentative skills. He is studying critical reasoning, and anyone who studies critical reasoning is bound to sharpen his argumentative skills.

   b. If your relationship with your spouse were based on fair exchanges, then it would be stable. It is not stable. Your relationship with your spouse is not based on fair exchanges.

   c. If Paul can find the strength to resist Sheila's advances, then he will be able to salvage some measure of self-respect. He will find this strength. He will salvage some self-respect.

   d. Anyone who deceives other people is guilty of a form of coercion. Anyone who deceives others is manipulating their choices. Anyone who manipulates the choices of others is guilty of a form of coercion.

   e. Your car doesn't have fuel. If it had fuel, it would have kept running. It didn't keep running.

   f. Alvin has not fulfilled the graduation requirements. If he has fulfilled the graduation requirements, then he is eligible for graduation. Alvin is not eligible for graduation.

   g. Any armed intervention should be entered only as a last resort. Any armed intervention has many innocent victims. Any activity that has many innocent victims should be entered only as a last resort.

   h. Students will not become more interested in learning for its own sake. Universities will become more vocationally oriented. Either students will become more interested in learning for its own sake or universities will become more vocationally oriented.

   i. If a human being is created at the moment of conception, then abortion always kills a human being. If abortion always kills a human being, then it is never justified. If a human being is created at the moment of conception, then abortion is never justified.

   j. Casual sex is justifiable in some cases. If some people can't find a partner who is willing to enter a serious relationship, casual sex is their only alternative to abstinence. Some people can't find a partner who is willing to enter a serious relationship. If casual sex is the only alternative to abstinence for some people, then casual sex is justifiable in some cases.

k. Roberta will eventually become desensitized to violence. Everyone who watches a lot of violent films eventually becomes desensitized to violence. Roberta watches a lot of violent films.

3. The following arguments don't exactly fit any of the seven patterns listed on the chart in this chapter. Try to determine their patterns. Identify the premises and conclusion and formulate the (new) patterns.

a. True conservatives resist spending for social programs. Our senator doesn't resist spending for social programs. Our senator is not a true conservative.

b. We shouldn't abolish capital punishment. If we do, prisons will become more crowded. If prisons become more crowded, then we will have to build more prisons. We don't want to build more prisons.

c. Some judges have been subjected to corrupting influences. Anyone who has practiced law has been subjected to corrupting influences. Some judges have practiced law.

d. If we limit welfare to a few years, then we must either guarantee health care to everyone, or we must be willing to let those taken off welfare go without health care. We have limited welfare to a few years. We are not willing to let those taken off welfare go without health care. We must guarantee health care to everyone.

e. Either you should take control of your own life or trust the advice of a mentor. If you trust the advice of a mentor, then you stand the risk of being used to fulfill the mentor's own dreams. You should not take that risk. You should take control of your own life.

Identifying Premises and Conclusions in Longer Passages

So far, we have presented short passages consisting entirely of premises and conclusions. In such cases, the task of identifying these argument parts is simplified—we know that one of the statements is the conclusion and the remaining ones are premises. If we don't see immediately which statement is the conclusion, we can go through a process of elimination trying each statement in that role and asking how well the remaining statements serve as support.

In longer passages, identifying premises and conclusions is more difficult and more a matter of interpretation. Even if the main purpose of a passage is to present an argument, most of the statements in it usually are neither premises nor conclusions. The passage displayed on page 39 is an adaptation of an editorial given in an exercise at the end of chapter 11. It contains several paragraphs from the original with the addition of several sentences that make the argument in the passage more explicit. Although it is still somewhat more complete than many argumentative passages found in actual editorials, it is quite typical in including a variety of statements that illustrate points, make reference to supporting sources, or restate elements in the argument.

Title suggests conclusion C

No Right to Cause Death

(Excerpt from *New York Times* editorial, January 10, 1993 with statements added in brackets to make the argument more explicit.)

The rationale for granting smokers the "right" to spread their toxic fumes around has disappeared. Diehards, egged on by the tobacco companies that supply them, have long tried to cast their habit as a civil liberties issue, claiming they should be free to engage in a practice that harms no one but themselves.

Another version of P_1

But the evidence is now overwhelming that smokers endanger all those forced to inhale the lethal clouds they generate. That makes smokers at least a small hazard to virtually all Americans—and a fitting target for tighter restrictions. . . .

The E.P.A. marshals an enormous array of evidence to build an overwhelming case that tobacco smoke is hazardous to innocent bystanders. The smoke that emanates from a smoldering cigarette contains virtually the same cancer-causing compounds as the smoke inhaled by the smokers. The inhaled smoke is known to cause cancer; it would be astonishing if the environmental smoke were not carcinogenic as well.

P_1

The main difference is that bystanders take in a more diluted mixture—they have no choice in the matter. Smoking does, therefore, involve the violation of rights, and it is the smokers who are the violators. . . . [If smoking poses a risk to the health of bystanders, then smoking violates their rights.]

Version of C

P_2

No one would grant his neighbor the right to blow tiny amounts of asbestos into a room or sprinkle traces of pesticide onto food. By the same logic, [if smoking violates the rights of bystanders, then] smokers have no right to spew even more noxious clouds into the air around them.

P_3

The unshaded statements from the passage constitute an argument. The conclusion is marked by a *C* in the margin and contains the conclusion indicator word *therefore*. The statements marked P_1, P_2, and P_3 are premises that support this conclusion.

In this case, the premises and conclusion fit together into one of the patterns on our chart of Some Common Successful Argument Patterns:[7]

Example 2.12

(1) *A.*

(2) *If A, then B.*

(3) *If B, then C.*

∴ *C.*

---

7. Note that this argument pattern, which we have called the *chain argument,* is fifth on the chart and can be seen as a combination of the first, *modus ponens,* and the fourth, *hypothetical syllogism.*

This argument form corresponds to the following rough interpretation:

Rough Interpretation

(1) Tobacco smoke is hazardous to innocent bystanders.

(2) If smoking poses a risk to the health of bystanders, then smoking violates their rights.

(3) If smoking violates the rights of bystanders, then smokers have no right to spew even more noxious clouds into the air around them.

∴ *Smokers have no right to cause death (that is, spew even more noxious clouds into the air around them).*

This interpretation of the argument is supported by other elements in the passage. As is indicated in the notes in the boxes on the left, the conclusion of the argument is suggested by the title, and another phrasing of premise 1 is given in the second paragraph. To put the argument into standard form in such a way that we follow the argument pattern given in Example 2.12 precisely, we need only paraphrase and slightly recast the rough interpretation.

More Formal Interpretation

(1) Smoking poses a risk to the health of innocent bystanders.

(2) If smoking poses a risk to the health of innocent bystanders, then smoking violates the rights of innocent bystanders.

(3) If smoking violates the rights of innocent bystanders, then smokers have no right to smoke around other people.

∴ *Smokers have no right to smoke around other people.*

The material in succeeding chapters will help you in interpreting longer passages. Use of indicator words as well as recognition of argument patterns will help you in carrying out this task. Passages found in editorials and other "real-world" contexts contain a variety of statements that are not essential (strictly speaking) to the presentation of an argument. They contain illustrations and references to sources as well as repetitions. Furthermore, as we will discuss in the next chapter, most of these passages do not explicitly contain all the elements needed to reconstruct an argument in standard form. The task of reconstruction is not purely "mechanical." You have to be prepared to discard many (in some cases most) of the statements in a passage to tease out an argument.

Exercise 2.4   **Reconstructing Explicit Arguments in Longer Passages**

Restate in standard form what you take to be the main argument put forth in the following passages. If you can, make the argument fit a pattern so that the conclusion follows from the premises. This may involve putting the premises and conclusion into your own words. You may need to rewrite your interpretation several times before it will fit into a concise pattern. (After you have worked on this individually, you might want to work with a group of other students, combining some of your insights to produce a better interpretation.)

1.

Guns and Free Discourse

The Second Amendment guarantee to bear arms is no less clear than the First Amendment guarantee of free expression. Gun control advocates overlook this similarity. Often the same person supports gun control but opposes censorship of controversial "art." But if gun control is constitutional, then it is also constitutional to restrict artistic expression.

The courts have consistently ruled that the Constitution assures adults freedom of expression. Even though some might be offended, it is not enough that people find a work distasteful. Our Constitution guarantees the right to produce and view it. So even though contemporary society suffers from too many guns, gun possession is similarly assured by our Constitution.

2.

Networks Don't Get Connection
(Excerpt from column by Cal Thomas
Seattle Post-Intelligencer, May 14, 1992)[8]

ABC Television broadcast a special "Men, Sex and Rape," . . . full of "pretension to virtue." . . . First Amendment absolutists have resisted every attempt to control the huge levels of effluent [from TV] that have turned our society into a toxic waste dump. . . . One does not have to be a social scientist to see a connection between increased incidents of rape, and other acts of violence against women, and the way women are treated in the popular media. . . . If rape is a terrible crime, and it is, and if there is a connection between pornography and the cultural permission it gives those already predisposed to perform these acts on women, then the government has an obligation and duty to control its proliferation.

---

8. The full, unmodified version of the editorial is given as an exercise at the end of chapter 4.

3.

Gender Tests May Not Be Worth Risk of Misuse
(Excerpt from column by Ellen Goodman, with statements added in brackets for clarification in this exercise)[9]

The woman beside me pats her rounded stomach and rolls her eyes to the ceiling, exclaiming, "Is she ever active today!" The "she" in this action won't be born until March. But my pregnant companion already knows the gender of this gestation.

I have grown accustomed to the attachment of a pronoun to a fetus by now. Most women I know of her age and anxiety level have had "the test" and gotten the results.

Over the past two decades, through amniocentesis and then CVS and sonograms, a generation of parents has received a prenatal exam, a genetic checkup on their offspring. They have all been given new information and sometimes new, unhappy choices. . . .

But this test may increase the possibility of abortion for sex selection by those who regard gender—the wrong gender—as a genetic flaw. . . .

It is the rare person who defends it on the grounds of population control or pure parental choice. It is a rarer American who chooses it. Indeed, the only countries in which sex selection occurs in discernible numbers have been those such as India or Korea where daughters have long been unwanted. It is almost always female fetuses that are aborted.

But gender testing and the capacity for gender choosing—before and after conception—is an ethical issue in this country, too. This is the first, but hardly the last time, that the new technology will be available to produce designer babies. Today, genetic testing is valued in America because it leads to the diagnosis of diseases that cause pain and death and disability. Eventually it may lead to their cure. But in the future, we also are likely to have access to much more information about genes than we need medically. We may be able to identify the gene for height, hair color, eye color, perhaps even athletic ability or intelligence. [America's fascination with technology suggests that we will not be able to resist the temptation to use this technology for sex selection.

If gender testing and gender choosing are permitted to become widely and easily available, then we must be able to resist using it.] At the moment, the moral consensus against sex selection is holding. . . . But in the longer run, the rest of us may be called upon to ask whether our curiosity about gender is worth the risk that others will misuse that information. [Consequently, programs of gender testing and choosing should not be permitted to become more broadly accessible.] It may be wiser to learn if the baby is a "he" or a "she" the old-fashioned way.

---

9. The full editorial is presented as an exercise in chapter 11.

 *CHAPTER THREE*

Understanding Arguments Through Reconstruction

Many of the examples considered in chapter 2 sound contrived because we don't usually hear or read arguments spelled out in such painful detail. Ordinary communication often assumes that the audience will be able to fill in the missing details. If you were discussing gender discrimination with a friend, for example, he might argue this:

Example 3.1

I don't care what you say; if it's wrong to discriminate against a woman on the basis of her gender, then it is equally wrong to discriminate against a man on the basis of his.

In this passage, there is no explicit conclusion, and a premise needed to complete the argument is missing.[1] In everyday discourse, arguments are often presented with implicit (that is, unstated) premises, and even implicit conclusions. In this chapter, we explain how the argument fragments that we commonly hear and read can be reconstructed so that their entire content, including implicit premises or conclusions, is explicitly displayed. In many situations such a full reconstruction is unnecessary. However, when you encounter complicated passages or seek to criticize an argument, it is often helpful to create such reconstructions. Once you have worked through some reconstruction exercises, you should find it easier to recognize what has been left implicit in fragmentary arguments, like the one stated in Example 3.1, even when you do not actually restate or rewrite the argument in reconstructed form. You are then in a better position to evaluate the assumptions or presuppositions behind the argument.

---

1. The argument omits the premise that it is wrong to discriminate against a woman on the basis of her gender and the conclusion that it is wrong to discriminate against a man on the basis of his gender.

Understanding Arguments by Identifying Implicit Conclusions

The least complicated case of reconstruction is one in which premises are supplied, with the audience left to "draw its own conclusion." In such circumstances the person offering an argument expects the context to make the conclusion clear. Suppose we hear a disc jockey giving this radio spot:

Example 3.2   *The smoother the sound, the better the station. The music is smoother at WARM radio.*

The obvious conclusion is that station WARM is better. In many cases like this, where only the conclusion is missing, the argument seems to point directly to the implicit conclusion.

Unfortunately, it isn't always so simple. Sometimes you might be in doubt about whether the conclusion of an argument is actually missing. In such a circumstance the technique of considering alternative readings, which was discussed in chapter 2, might help. Consider the following example:

Example 3.3   *If most American voters recognize that the cost of medical care is out of control, then the government will act. But everyone who has elderly relatives recognizes that the cost of medical care is out of control. And most American voters have elderly relatives.*

This passage has something to do with government response to rising medical costs. The passage does not, however, give many hints about its conclusion. We might begin by treating each of the three statements as the conclusion of the argument.

Reading 1   *(1) If most American voters recognize that the cost of medical care is out of control, then the government will act.*

(2) Everyone who has elderly relatives recognizes that the cost of medical care is out of control.

∴ *Most American voters have elderly relatives.*

Reading 2   *(1) If most American voters recognize that the cost of medical care is out of control, then the government will act.*

(2) Most American voters have elderly relatives.

∴ *Everyone who has elderly relatives recognizes that the cost of medical care is out of control.*

Reading 3   *(1) Everyone who has elderly relatives recognizes that the cost of medical care is out of control.*

(2) Most American voters have elderly relatives.

∴ *If most American voters recognize that the cost of medical care is out of control, then the government will act.*

Think about the meaning of the premises and conclusion in each case. *Does the conclusion follow from the premises?* In reading 1, for instance, the premises offer no reason for believing that "most American voters have elderly relatives." Although this statement might follow from the premises in some *other* argument, the premises supplied here are irrelevant. In each of the other readings, the premises also fail to give reasons that adequately support the conclusion. Such a mechanical process of developing alternative readings for an argument might seem overly cumbersome, but working through it a few times will help you begin to get a feel for argument structure and to sharpen your sense of whether a conclusion has been explicitly stated or left implicit.

Because in this case we have found that the conclusion is not explicitly stated, our next step is to formulate the implicit conclusion. To discover the hidden conclusion that the premises support, you will often find it useful to list the premises.

Reading 4   *(1) If most American voters recognize that the cost of medical care is out of control, then the government will act.*

(2) Everyone who has elderly relatives recognizes that the cost of medical care is out of control.

(3) Most American voters have elderly relatives.

∴ *???*

Think about what statement these premises jointly support and how they are linked. The second and third premises together support the statement that most American voters recognize that the cost of medical care is out of control. This taken with the first premise supports the conclusion of the entire argument: "The government will act."

Reading 4 illustrates two important features of a good reconstruction for arguments with missing elements. First, it strives, *other things being equal,*[2] to interpret the argument in such a way that *the conclusion does indeed follow from the premises.* In this reading the conclusion follows from the premises, whereas in each of the other three readings, the supposed conclusion does not follow from the premises.

---

2. Other things are *not* equal if the passage actually suggests a reading in which the conclusion does not follow from the premises.

Further, it is difficult to find acceptable implicit premises that could be used to support these "conclusions." Second, the argument *uses all stated premises*. Notice the way reading 4 uses all three premises to support the conclusion and compare this reading with the following reading, which makes some of the premises contained in the passage unnecessary:

Reading 5

(1) *If most American voters recognize that the cost of medical care is out of control, then the government will act.*

(implicit)

(2) *If the government acts, then the reputation of the Congress will be enhanced.*

(implicit)

∴ *If most American voters recognize that the cost of medical care is out of control, then the reputation of the Congress will be enhanced.*

Reading 5 does not use all the available material in the passage. It picks out one element as a premise, disregards the rest, and reaches a conclusion that is not even hinted at in the passage. Of course, in order to do so, an implicit premise also needs to be added. In chapter 2 we encouraged applying the Principle of Charitable Interpretation, but attributing an argument that is not even suggested by the text is not providing an *interpretation* that is charitable, even if the argument is a good one.

Understanding Arguments by Identifying Implicit Premises

More common than the argument with an implicit conclusion is the argument that presents a conclusion and some of the premises needed to support it but leaves out one or more statements necessary to guarantee the truth of the conclusion. These missing premises are sometimes referred to as *assumptions* or *presuppositions* of the argument.[3] Consider this example:

Example 3.4

A law that would reduce the blood alcohol limit for driving is a bad idea, because anything that would put ordinary social drinkers in jail is a bad idea.

The indicator word *because* flags the second statement in this sentence as a premise and the first as the conclusion. In standard form we have:

Reconstruction 1

(1) *Anything that would put ordinary social drinkers in jail is a bad idea.*

∴ *A law that would reduce the blood alcohol limit for driving is a bad idea.*

---

3. We might distinguish between an assumption and a presupposition this way: calling the missing premise an *assumption* interprets it as a position that is likely held but not stated by the arguer, whereas to call it a *presupposition* allows that the author of the argument may be unaware that this premise is required.

What is missing in this argument is the assumption that links the stated premise to the conclusion. As the argument is now written, it is assumed that a law that would reduce the blood alcohol limit for driving would put ordinary social drinkers in jail, an assumption that might well be doubted. This assumption is made explicit in the following version of the argument, which is easier to understand and to criticize.

Reconstruction 2

(implicit)

(1) Anything that would put ordinary social drinkers in jail is a bad idea.

(2) A law that would reduce the blood alcohol limit for driving would put ordinary social drinkers in jail.

∴ *A law that would reduce the blood alcohol limit for driving is a bad idea.*

Sometimes the missing premise is an assumption about the definition of some term in the argument. For example:

Example 3.5

Abortion involves intentionally taking the life of an innocent person, so abortion is murder.

What is missing here is a statement that characterizes *intentionally taking the life of an innocent person* as *murder.* Once this definitional assumption is made explicit, it is apparent that the conclusion follows from the premises.

The implicit premise in itself is not very controversial, although the argument might provoke debate.[4] Indeed, if you have a choice in adding implicit elements to an argument reconstruction, *the more plausible, less questionable statements should be selected.* In the argument in Example 3.5, for instance, the conclusion would still follow if we added a premise that the taking of a human life constituted murder, irrespective of whether it was done intentionally or involved an innocent person. But in the context of the passage, which includes the words *intentionally* and *innocent,* such a reading would not be charitable.

Although the Principle of Charitable Interpretation enjoins us to add the most reasonable implicit premises or conclusions that can be plausibly attributed to the author, given what is stated in the passage, it need not be one that *we* believe is true. In fact, one of the advantages of reconstructing an argument is that we sometimes expose a hidden premise that is controversial, as in Example 3.6:

Example 3.6

Stealing is wrong. Using a friend's car without asking is taking property without permission. So using a friend's car without asking is wrong.

The implicit premise needed to reconstruct this passage can be stated: *Taking property without permission is (always) stealing.* This premise is, at best, doubtful. Special

---

4. The explicit premise would probably be the focus of concern because it is true only if we consider the fetus to be a full-fledged person. If not (as some maintain), then it is false to say that abortion involves taking the life of an innocent *person.*

circumstances, such as an emergency or the absence of any intention to keep the car, suggest that sometimes taking property without asking permission is not an act of stealing.

Reconstruction

(1) *Stealing is wrong.*

(2) *Using a friend's car without asking is taking property without permission.*

(implicit)

(3) *Taking property without permission is stealing.*

———

∴ *Using a friend's car without asking is wrong.*

Adding Both Conclusion and Premises

There are also cases in which both the conclusion and some of the premises are missing. In such cases the best way to begin is to supply what appears to be the intended conclusion and then to consider the premises needed as plausible assumptions to support it. In making this reconstruction, it is helpful to pay close attention to the context, as you can see in the following example:

Example 3.7

Those who fear the future have misled us. If Americans will mobilize the forces that have made them great, then they will ultimately weather the problem of global economic competitiveness and develop effective new products and manufacturing techniques to meet the challenge.

The editorial comment that those who fear the future have misled us indicates that the author would assert a conclusion that is not one of fear. The second clause of the next sentence—"they will ultimately weather the problem of global economic competitiveness"—offers hope, suggesting that this is the author's intended conclusion. This first step in reconstruction yields:

Reading 1

(1) *If Americans will mobilize the forces that have made them great, then they will ultimately weather the problem of global economic competitiveness and develop effective new products and manufacturing techniques to meet the challenge.*

(implicit)

———

∴ *Americans will ultimately weather the problem of global economic competitiveness and develop effective new products and manufacturing techniques to meet the challenge.*

What is missing from this formulation is the hidden assumption that Americans will indeed mobilize the forces that have made them great. The Principle of Charitable Interpretation directs us to understand the argument in this more fully developed way.

Reading 2

(1) *If Americans will mobilize the forces that have made them great, then they will ultimately weather the problem of global economic competitiveness and develop effective new products and manufacturing techniques to meet the challenge.*

(implicit)

(2) *Americans will mobilize the forces that have made them great.*

(implicit)

∴ *Americans will ultimately weather the problem of global economic competitiveness and develop effective new products and manufacturing techniques to meet the challenge.*

The implicit premise—premise 2—is the most controversial part of the argument. Only when it is made explicit can we criticize the contention effectively.

Guidelines and Warnings in Adding Implicit Premises and Conclusions

Our discussion of the Principle of Charitable Interpretation in chapter 2 suggests guidelines for reconstructing arguments with missing elements. The following general rules apply when there is no *explicit* evidence to the contrary.

Guidelines for Reconstruction

Within the limits of faithfulness to the text, the reconstructed argument should:
1. Arrive at a conclusion that follows from the premises
2. Avoid false or highly questionable premises
3. Include all premises that are explicitly stated or strongly suggested[5]
   (These may need to be rephrased in ways that make the entire argument fit into a pattern.)
4. Include implicit premises that bring out underlying assumptions or presuppositions in a way that promotes critical discussion
   Note: To follow all the guidelines at once, you must balance content and structure. An argument must be complete, but a statement or assumption cannot be included as part of the argument if it isn't connected to the other premises in a way that leads to the conclusion. Achieving this balance is to some extent an art. It requires practice.

---

5. Often in "real-life" passages that contain arguments, much of the material serves other purposes than directly presenting the argument. Not every sentence corresponds to a premise or a conclusion; indeed, most do not. Hence, a good reconstruction *excludes all irrelevant material.* Nevertheless, some of the material—like illustrations or even the title—gives useful hints about the missing premise or conclusion.

We followed these guidelines in our reconstructions in the previous sections. But our comments relied on a general understanding of the passages and a feel for the structure of arguments. Sometimes our insights into arguments fail us initially, particularly when passages are complicated. Fortunately, there is a more mechanical process that can help in some cases. It takes advantage of the search for structure we described in chapter 2.

To apply guideline 1, a useful first step is to determine the structure of the argument as best we can. If we can see the argument as an instance of a successful argument pattern, we can get a better picture of what is needed to make the conclusion follow from the premises. Suppose we read the following selection from an essay in a magazine:

Example 3.8   *Television programming has become segregated: there are separate programs for and about blacks, whites, and Hispanics, with little overlap. The NAACP blames the networks for this situation, but the fault lies more with us than with the studios. Programming decisions are based on viewing habits and marketing. If segregated television continues to be aired, then we the public are choosing to watch it.*[6]

In this passage, the if-then structure of the last sentence can be recognized as occurring in some of the argument patterns discussed in chapter 2. But this sentence ("If segregated television continues to be aired, then we the public are choosing to watch it.") needs to be connected with the rest of the passage. The first sentence suggests that the author would assert the "if" part of the "if-then" sentence to be true. The claim that although the NAACP blames segregated television on the studios, "the fault lies more with us than with the studios," suggests that the passage is presenting reasons why we, the public, deserve most of the blame for segregated television. If we put these elements together, we have the partial reconstruction:

Partial
Reconstruction

(1) Segregated television continues to be aired.

(2) If segregated television continues to be aired, then the public is choosing to watch it.

∴ *The public deserves most of the blame for segregated television.*

This reconstruction has the structure

(1) A.

(2) If A, then B.

∴ *C.*

---

6. Adapted from Tamar Jacoby, "Adjust Your Sets," *The New Republic,* 24 January 2000.

which we can recognize as needing the additional premise *If B, then C* to complete the pattern of the chain argument.

(1) A.

(2) If A, then B.

(3) If B, then C.

∴ *C.*

This allows us to complete the reconstruction of the argument.

Full Reconstruction

(1) Segregated television continues to be aired.

(2) If segregated television continues to be aired, then the public is choosing to watch it.

(3) If the public is choosing to watch it, then the public deserves most of the blame for segregated television.

∴ *The public deserves most of the blame for segregated television.*

These steps in using patterns to help reconstruct arguments are summarized in the box below.

As with all the Guidelines for Reconstruction, the recommendation to try to reconstruct the argument as an instance of a successful argument pattern provides only general criteria for evaluating alternative reconstructions. It cannot be followed blindly. For some arguments or argument fragments, there is no way, *faithful to the text,* that allows us to reconstruct them so that the conclusion follows from the premises.

Using Patterns to Reconstruct Arguments

1. Look for structuring words or word pairs like *if . . . then, either . . . or, not, all,* or *every;* look as well for statements or parts of statements that are repeated.
2. Write out the partial pattern for the portion of the argument that is stated.
3. Determine what the complete pattern is.
4. From the part of the pattern that is missing, determine what statements are missing.

Notice that there is an *overly easy* way of adding a premise to complete any argument. It should be used only as a last resort. Let's use the following example of a partially reconstructed argument:

Example 3.9

(1) *No one who wants fame can be trusted.*

(2) *Edward is a journalist.*

∴ *Edward can't be trusted.*

It is always possible to write an if-then premise that connects the premises already stated with the conclusion. Using this procedure, we can complete Example 3.9 in this manner:

Easy Way of Completing Example 3.9 (implicit)

(1) *No one who wants fame can be trusted.*

(2) *Edward is a journalist.*

(3) *If no one who wants fame can be trusted and Edward is a journalist, then Edward can't be trusted.*

∴ *Edward can't be trusted.*

Using the easy way, we have made premises 1 and 2 into the "if" part of our added premise, and the conclusion into the "then" part. However, there is an alternative way of completing Example 3.9 that adheres more closely to guideline 4 from the list on page 49.

Preferred Way of Completing Example 3.9 (implicit)

(1) *No one who wants fame can be trusted.*

(2) *Edward is a journalist.*

(3) *All journalists want fame.*

∴ *Edward can't be trusted.*

This latter formulation is better because it states more specifically what is presupposed in the argument of Example 3.9. If you were to criticize the argument, the preferred reconstruction would direct you to scrutinize the claim that all journalists want fame. With the easy if-then reconstruction, you can see only that the argument presupposes some connection between the stated premises and the conclusion, but it is not clear what this connection is. The if-then premise— premise 3—simply restates the argument of Example 3.9 in a single sentence. You can just as easily question whether the conclusion of the argument follows from the premises as you can whether the if-then implicit premise is true. For this reason, the "easy" reconstruction violates guideline 4 because it does *not* bring out underlying presuppositions in a way that promotes critical discussion.

Picking out an *interesting, not overly easy,* implicit premise was relatively straight-forward for the partially reconstructed argument in Example 3.9. But deciding what implicit premise to add in reconstruction in less stylized contexts can be a greater problem. If Example 3.9 were an argument embedded in a passage that focused on TV news becoming more like sensationalist, "tabloid" journalism, we might have added this to premise 2 and modified the implicit premise 3 to take this into account:

(modified)   *(2') Edward is a "tabloid" journalist.*

(implicit)   *(3') All "tabloid" journalists want fame.*

Alternatively, if the argument were embedded in a context that discussed the cut-throat competition in the market in which Edward worked, then another version of the implicit premises would be appropriate:

(modified)   *(2") Edward is a journalist in a cutthroat market.*

(implicit)   *(3") All journalists in a cutthroat market want fame.*

Notice that implicit premise 3 makes the boldest claim. It applies to "all journal-ists." The other two—3' and 3"—make less bold statements about all journalists of a certain type or working in a certain kind of market. These qualifications might make one version of a prospective implicit premise more defensible than another. If, however, the passage gives no hint about such a more qualified ver-sion, then you are not required by the guidelines to supply it. At a certain point, the burden of clearly stating the argument falls on its author.

There is *no simple formula* for selecting which version of an implicit premise to include. Sometimes elements of the passage will suggest which version is more appropriate. Other times you will need to rely on the Principle of Charitable Inter-pretation and pick the version that seems most acceptable from among those that can be plausibly attributed to the author.

Exercise 3.1   **Recognizing Argument Patterns and Adding Implicit Premises, Conclusions, or Both**

This exercise should help prepare you to identify premises and conclusions that are left unstated. It will give you practice in learning to apply the steps in Using Patterns to Reconstruct Arguments (p. 51) as well as the Guidelines for Reconstruction (p. 49). When it is not immediately obvious what premise or conclusion has been left unstated, identifying the pattern of the argument can be helpful.

1. Fill in the blanks and indicate the argument pattern given below.

Sample:

Suppose you are trying to identify the missing premise in this argument:

(1) If Dan lied, then he kept the money for himself.

(2) [_____ *.]*

∴ *Dan didn't lie.*

As indicated in the box on page 51, to identify the pattern of an argument, look for words or word pairs like *if . . . then, either . . . or,* or *not,* and look for statements or parts of statements that are repeated in the argument. If we substitute *A* for *Dan lied* and *B* for *he [Dan] kept the money for himself,* we can represent the argument with the following "partial" pattern:

(1) If A, then B.

(2) [_____ *.]*

∴ *Not A.*

Now compare this partial pattern to the list of complete patterns in chapter 2. Our partial pattern is a fragment of the following complete pattern:

(1) If A, then B.

(2) Not B. _____

∴ *Not A.*

The implicit premise, then, is: *Not B.* To put this into an English sentence, you have to find what *B* stands for in premise 1 and then deny that sentence. In this case, premise 2 is: *Dan did not keep the money for himself.* You could insert this in the sample above.

Write patterns here.

Go through steps 1–4 in the box on page 51 for the following problems. We have helped you by filling in key words in some of the missing premises and conclusions.

a. *(1) If the Netwizard desktop computer runs Webvideo software, then it can meet my computing needs.*

(2) [_____ *].*

∴ *The Netwizard desktop computer can meet my computing needs.*

b. *(1) Either [* _____ *]*
or I should buy the Hacker laptop:

(2) I shouldn't buy the Netwizard desktop computer. _____

∴ *I should buy the Hacker laptop.*

c. *(1) If the Hacker laptop does not run Webvideo software, then I can't play intertactive webvideo games on it.*

   (2) If [   ]
      then [   ]

   ∴ *If the Hacker laptop does not run Webvideo software, then it doesn't meet my needs.*

d. *(1) If David can afford a new plasma high-definition TV, then [   ]*

   (2) David can't afford to pay off his credit card debts.

   ∴ *David can't afford a new plasma high-definition TV.*

e. *(1) Either [   ] or [   ].*

   (2) I shouldn't buy a Econoplasma high-definition TV.

   ∴ *I should buy a Primeoview high-definition TV.*

f. *(1) If the Hacker laptop has only 128 Megs of RAM, then [   ].*

   (2) If it can't run Webvideo software, then I shouldn't buy it.

   (3) [   ].

   ∴ *I shouldn't buy it.*

g.[7] *(1) All primeoview high-definition plasma TVs are products guaranteed for three years.*

   (2) All [   ] are [   ].

   ∴ *All primeoview high-definition plasma TVs are products that give you a lot of protection against faulty engineering and workmanship.*

---

7. Fill the slots in exercises g and h with words that apply to classes of objects (for example, "high-definition plasma TVs") or that designate a particular object belonging to a class (for example, "my new high-definition plasma TV"). Do not insert a complete sentence into the slots for these exercises.

h. *(1) Any addition to my TV entertainment system is an extravagance.*

(2) [   ] is [   ].

∴ A new high-definition plasma TV is an extravagance.

Write patterns here. The following exhibit more complicated patterns, not listed in chapter 2. Can you figure out the patterns they exhibit?

i. *(1) If the Netwizard desktop computer can run Webvideo software, and it is cheaper than the Hacker laptop, then I should buy it.*

(2) [   ]

(3) [   ]

∴ I should buy the Netwizard desktop computer.

j. *(1) Either I'll spend my bonus on a new plasma high-definition TV, or I'll repair my car (but not both).*

(2) If I do not repair my car, then I risk a serious accident.

(3) [   ].

∴ I won't spend my bonus on a new plasma high-definition TV.

k. *(1) Either I should buy more books or more Xbox games.*

(2) If this money was given to me for my education, then I should not buy more Xbox games.

(3) [   ].

∴ I should buy more books.

2. Put the following arguments into standard form. Add implicit premises and conclusions. Leave out any editorial comments. For problems a–k, indicate the argument pattern, using letters to represent repeated elements.

   a. You promised to be here at 8:00. If you promised to be here at 8:00, then you should have arrived at 8:00.

   b. I should either study more or prepare to accept failure. I should study more.

    c. If you tell lies frequently, then you must remember not only what you have done but also what you said you have done. Therefore, if you tell lies frequently, your memory becomes burdened.

    d. Harold should be sensitive to other people because any teacher should be sensitive to other people.

    e. American universities are eroding their public support. Any social institution that spends beyond the willingness of the public to pay is eroding its public support.

    f. If being affectionate were the only important virtue, then Maurice would be a saint. So being affectionate is obviously not the only important virtue.

    g. We will face substantial energy shortages by the year 2020 because there are not enough alternative fuel facilities under construction. *(Note:* Sometimes there is no alternative to adding the easy linking premise: *"If premise 1, then conclusion.")*

    h. Many college faculty members are reaching retirement age. But if that is so, then many new, younger faculty members will be hired. It follows that, before long, college faculties will become more energetic.

    i. Every successful politician has to compromise his principles occasionally. Everyone who has to compromise his principles occasionally loses integrity.

    j. The number of unmarried adults in the United States is continuing to increase. If there is an increase in people unsupported by close personal bonds, there will be an increase in alcoholism and suicide. So there will be an increase in alcoholism and suicide.

    k. The current generation in their 20s has a chance at avoiding impoverishment if the baby boom generation and those over sixty limit the deficit. If the older generation really accepts its responsibility for the future, it will limit the deficit. The generation in power is now beginning to realize its obligation to posterity, so the conclusion is clear.

Passages l–q do not fit into the common patterns of argument we have considered previously. Reconstruct them in standard form.

    l. The higher the interest rates, the better the bank. The interest rates at CASH National Bank are the highest in town.

    m. Apparently you don't smoke opium, since everyone who smokes opium is happy.

    n. Either I should spend my tax refund on paying off my debts or I should buy books for this term. But if I don't buy books, I'll risk failing my courses. So I shouldn't spend the refund on paying off my debts.

    o. It looks like Bruce will get a promotion. Alice has a great new job in Minneapolis. If so, she'll be moving, and that will create an opening for either Bruce or Frank.

    p. Every human action is determined by laws of nature. But for a person to deserve praise or blame, it is necessary for the person to have been able to act differently than she in fact did act. So no person deserves praise or blame.

q. The industrialized nations will resolve the environmental crises that are looming in the near future if these nations mobilize all the technological resources at their disposal. If political incentives are sufficiently high, then the mobilization of resources will occur. Public awareness about oil spills, depletion of the ozone layer, and the "greenhouse effect" is growing rapidly. If so, political incentives are sufficiently high. The conclusion is clear.

In the following passages much of what is stated is either not part of the argument or must be restated to make the structure of the argument clear. There may be more than one acceptable reconstruction.

r. As we all know, the American public is reluctant to try any new approach to education that might erode support for public schools. But the problems of education in inner cities have become so critical that there is little to lose. Either we give the voucher system and charter schools a fair trial, or we abandon the potential of the children of inner cities to become educated.

s. If a bad social environment causes people to become criminals, then everyone from a bad social environment would be a criminal. But for every criminal who comes from a bad social environment, there are thousands who hold jobs.

t. We have before us the question of rights for homosexuals—a question which I hope disturbs you as much as it does me. My friends, I am as much concerned about other people as anyone. But I am opposed to these so-called rights. The reason is that if the United States passed rights for homosexuals, then the United States would support what is unnatural. But the United States should never support what is unnatural.

3. Use the Guidelines for Reconstruction to determine which, if any, of the reconstructions provided are adequate for the passages given. Indicate why you reject the reconstructions you do. If you find all of them faulty, supply one yourself.

a. *Passage*

Either we should permanently cut taxes or we should use this opportunity to preserve Social Security and expand medical coverage. If we cut taxes now, we will be unable to fund these programs when the need inevitably arises. The conclusion is clear.

Reconstructions

i. *(1) Either we should permanently cut taxes, or we should use this opportunity to preserve Social Security and expand medical coverage.*

(2) We shouldn't preserve Social Security and expand medical coverage.

∴ *We should permanently cut taxes.*

ii. *(1) Either we should permanently cut taxes, or we should use this opportunity to preserve Social Security and expand medical coverage.*

   (2) If we permanently cut taxes now, we will be unable to fund Social Security and expanded medical coverage when the need inevitably arises.

   (3) We should not be unable to fund Social Security and expanded medical coverage when the need inevitably arises.

   ∴ *We should use this opportunity to preserve Social Security and expand medical coverage.*

iii. *(1) We should preserve Social Security and expand medical coverage.*

    (2) We have an obligation to those who paid into Social Security, and it would be inhumane to leave our citizens without medical insurance.

    ∴ *We shouldn't permanently cut taxes.*

b. *Passage*

I don't care what you say: if it's wrong to discriminate against a woman on the basis of her gender, then it is equally wrong to discriminate against a man on the basis of his. Permitting combat roles in the military for men only is unjust.

Reconstructions

i. *(1) If gender discrimination is wrong, then combat roles for men only are unjust.*

   (2) Combat roles for men only are unjust.

   ∴ *Gender discrimination is wrong.*

ii. *(1) If it is wrong to discriminate against a woman on the basis of her gender, then it is equally wrong to discriminate against a man on the basis of his.*

   (2) Combat roles for men only discriminate against a man on the basis of his gender.

   ∴ *Combat roles for men only are unjust.*

iii. *(1) If gender discrimination against women is wrong, then it is unjust to discriminate against a man on the basis of his gender.*

(2) Gender discrimination against women is wrong.

∴ *Combat roles for men only are unjust.*

c. *Passage*

Since Mervin has devoted himself to becoming a famous journalist, you should be careful what you tell him.

Reconstructions

i.   *(1) If Mervin has devoted himself to becoming a famous journalist, you should be careful what you tell him.*

   (2) Mervin has devoted himself to becoming a famous journalist.

   ∴ *You should be careful what you tell Mervin.*

ii.   *(1) If Mervin has devoted himself to becoming a famous journalist, all people should be careful what they tell him.*

   (2) Mervin has devoted himself to becoming a famous journalist.

   ∴ *All people should be careful what they tell Mervin.*

iii.   *(1) Everyone should be careful what they tell anybody who wants to become a famous journalist.*

   (2) Mervin has devoted himself to becoming a famous journalist.

   ∴ *Everyone should be careful what they tell Mervin.*

d. *Passage*

Reliance on abortion as a means of birth control will cheapen the American social commitment to protecting life. It should be banned except when the mother's life is in danger.

Reconstructions

i.   *(1) If reliance on abortion as a means of birth control will cheapen the American social commitment to protecting life, then it should be banned except when the mother's life is in danger.*

   (2) Reliance on abortion as a means of birth control will cheapen the American social commitment to protecting life.

   ∴ *Abortion should be banned except when the mother's life is in danger.*

ii. *(1) Anything that cheapens the American social commitment to protecting life should be banned.*

(2) Abortion as a means of birth control cheapens the American social commitment to protecting life.

∴ *Abortion should be banned.*

iii. *(1) Anything that cheapens the American social commitment to protecting life should be banned.*

(2) Except when the mother's life is in danger, abortion cheapens the American social commitment to protecting life.

∴ *Abortion should be banned except when the mother's life is in danger.*

Moving to Real-World Discourse

In passages that contain a good deal of argumentative material, it is often surprisingly difficult to determine exactly what point an author is trying to make. We briefly alluded to this problem in chapter 2. You might face difficulty, for instance, in finding the conclusion in the midst of all the other statements in the passage. Furthermore, the distinction between explicit and implicit premises and conclusions is not always sharp. A premise or conclusion can be strongly suggested but not stated precisely. You will seldom be able to copy a series of sentences from a passage and say, "These are the premises and the conclusion."

Even if, using indicator words and seeing the structure of an argument, you find a sentence that plays the role of the conclusion, you might not initially understand what the author means by it and how the premises support it. What does the author mean in the following passage?

Example 3.10

Social scientists have rightly held that people who are intermeshed in a network of overlapping, mutually supportive interpersonal relations and the concomitant commitment to common norms obtain a substantial measure of psychic support. This psychological fortification in turn limits the incidence of self-destructive and other deviant behavior. It follows that individuals with a high degree of involvement with the religious life of their community are less likely to be found on the lists of those who have taken the last fateful step to terminate their sojourn in this vale of tears.

Looking at the Context   When you are trying to understand an unclear passage, it is often useful to look at the context in which it appears. Is the passage part of an article whose main point is stated in the title? If so, how is the passage in question related to this point? Is the passage part of a debate in which the participants have clearly indicated which side they are supporting? If so, perhaps the passage is stating premises in support of one of the positions. If the passage in Example 3.10 were from a book, and it occurred in a chapter titled "Religion and Suicide," you could look for some point about the relation between religion and suicide. This additional information doesn't tell you specifically what the passage means, but it prepares you to focus your attention in a certain direction as you read through it.

Simplifying and Paraphrasing   To cut through the net of confusion created by passages such as the one in Example 3.10, it is helpful, after noting the context, to simplify and paraphrase. Once inessential elements are removed or modified, you can more readily grasp the structure of what is being said. Furthermore, a sign of whether you have mastered an argument is your ability to repeat what is meant—not merely the words used. This is a good test of understanding.

The task of simplifying and paraphrasing is not easy. The aim is to change an author's words without distorting the meaning of what was said. It is all the more difficult if you do not clearly understand what the author is saying. *Successive approximation* is a useful tactic. Begin with a rough (perhaps somewhat inaccurate) rendition of the passage. Then, if necessary, modify it in successive versions until it accurately reflects the original. In the process you will "make the author's argument your own" and understand it much better.

A First Approximation   The conclusion in Example 3.10 is indicated by the expression "it follows" in the final sentence, but its meaning is far from clear. Once the conclusion is located, a three-step process will help generate a first approximation:

1. *Penetrate the Prose*. Look up the words you don't know in a dictionary; decipher the meaning of metaphors and of vague, emotional, or flowery language; substitute more precise expressions.
     Sample: The conclusion of the example uses the fancy phrase "those who have taken the last fateful step to terminate their sojourn in this vale of tears" which means roughly "those who committed suicide."

2. *Eliminate the Excess*. Delete all editorial expressions or unnecessary clauses, and rephrase what remains in a straightforward way.
     Sample: The introductory comment "Social scientists have rightly held" should be removed.

3. *Search Out the Structure*. Figure out which statements provide support for the conclusion. If necessary, sketch the argument in such a way that the structure is clear.

   The argument can be sketched:

First Approximation

(1) *People with many friends feel more secure.*

(2) *Feeling secure makes people less suicidal.*

(implicit)   *(3) Churchgoers have many friends.*

                      ∴ *Churchgoers are less suicidal.[8]*

When you reconstruct a passage it is important to make a bold beginning. Don't be afraid to produce a very rough approximation. It is better to produce a parody that you truly understand than a parroting of the author's words that you do not. You can always revise your simplified version if you decide that you have weakened or significantly altered what the author is saying.

A Second Approximation

Our first approximation is much clearer than the original, but it is an oversimplification that is probably more open to criticism than the original. For example, it is an overgeneralization to say that churchgoers have many friends, and the passage doesn't make this bold a claim. It was worthwhile to put it this way in the first approximation because it is a simple, clear statement that connects the conclusion with the premises. If we go through our first approximation and qualify each sentence so it is closer to the original (but stated clearly), we arrive at something like the following:

(1) People who share a network of relationships and norms feel more secure.

(2) Feeling secure limits self-destructive behavior.

(3) People highly involved in religious life are likely to share a network of relationships and norms.

∴ *People highly involved in religious life are less likely to commit suicide.*

Even though this second approximation is more accurate, it is important to go through the initial step of oversimplifying the passage. This helps you move beyond reciting the words of the passage as you would recite words in a poem you have memorized but don't understand. By oversimplifying the passage you take over the thought as if it were your own. You can always go back and qualify.

Exercise 3.2   **Simplification and Paraphrasing: Making a First Approximation**

Simplify and paraphrase the following passages. Try to capture the basic meaning as economically as you can. For the first approximation do not hesitate to substantially

---

8. We could go a step further and put these sentences into an if-then pattern—for example, by writing the first premise as *If people have many friends, then they feel more secure than people without many friends.*

rewrite the passage and to eliminate less important elements. Most of the passages are not arguments.

1. Few are the rewards of indolence and many its pains; rich is the harvest of hard work.

2. If you want to get ahead in this world, you've got to be down at the carwash when the fancy cars roll in.

3. Only by cleaving firmly to the bosom of the land can the new pioneer escape the soul-crushing forces of modern, technological society.

4. A full-bodied network of communication is necessary for any officeholder if he or she is to effectively transform crucial, but unexciting, behind-the-scenes work into the forge that will produce results at the polls.

5. Success in teaching rests on three interrelated factors: (1) A teacher must have that easy familiarity that betokens the true participant in the life of the mind; (2) a teacher must be involved in a give-and-take of communication with the student so that the student is motivated and the teacher is apprised of the student's needs; and finally (3) a teacher must be able to evaluate both the student's progress and potential without bias brought about by the teacher's own successes and failures in the classroom.

6. To UNDERSTAND political power right and derive it from its original, we must consider what state all men are naturally in, and that is a state of perfect freedom to order their actions and dispose of their possessions and persons as they think fit, within the bounds of the law of nature, without asking leave or depending upon the will of any other man.[9]

7. Yet all this bespeaks a dim realization of the truth—the truth that modern man lives under the illusion that he knows what he wants, while he actually wants what he is *supposed* to want. In order to accept this it is necessary to realize that to know what one really wants is not comparatively easy, as most people think, but one of the most difficult problems any human being has to solve. It is a task we frantically try to avoid by accepting ready-made goals as though they were our own.[10] **(Hint: Does Fromm believe that people really know what they want?)**

8. It would seem that the obstacles to generalized thought inherent in the form of language are of minor importance only, and that presumably the language alone would not prevent a people from advancing to more generalized forms of thinking if the general state of their culture should require expression of such thought; that under these conditions the language would be molded

---

9. John Locke, *The Second Treatise of Government*, ed. Thomas Peardon (New York: Bobbs-Merrill, 1952), 4.

10. Erich Fromm, *Escape from Freedom* (New York: Avon, 1967), 278.

rather by the cultural state. It does not seem likely, therefore, that there is any direct relation between the culture of a tribe and the language they speak, except insofar as the form of language will be molded by the state of culture, but not insofar as a certain state of culture is conditioned by morphological traits of the language.[11] **(Hint: What does Boas say about the relation among language, thought, and culture?)**

9. No age in the history of humanity has perhaps so lost touch with this natural *healing* process that implicates *some* of the people whom we label schizophrenic. No age has so devalued it, no age has imposed such prohibitions and deterrences against it, as our own. Instead of the mental hospital, a sort of reservicing factory for human breakdowns, we need a place where people who have traveled further and, consequently, may be more lost than psychiatrists and other sane people, can find their way further into inner space and time, and back again. Instead of the *degradation* ceremonial of psychiatric examination, diagnosis, and prognostication, we need, for those who are ready for it (in psychiatric terminology, often those who are about to go into a schizophrenic breakdown), an *initiation* ceremonial, through which the person will be guided with full social encouragement and sanction into inner space and time, by people who have been there and back again. Psychiatrically, this would appear as ex-patients helping future patients go mad.[12] **(Hint: Concentrate on the virtue Laing sees in the alternative rather than on the liabilities of traditional psychiatric practice.)**

10. If information is power, the ability to distort and control information will be used more often than not to preserve and perpetuate that power. But the national security policy makers, the crisis managers of the nuclear age, are frequently men of considerable intellectual ability who have gone to the right schools. They pride themselves not only on their social graces, but on their rationality and morality. For such men, the preservation of partisan political power would not be a seemly rationale for official deception (although it might be entirely sufficient for the President whom they serve). National security provides the acceptable alternative, the end that justifies all means. . . . The excuse for secrecy and deception most frequently given by those in power is that the American people must sometimes be misled in order to mislead the enemy. This justification is unacceptable on moral and philosophical grounds, and often it simply isn't true. Frequently, the "enemy" knows what is going on, but the American public does not.[13] **(Hint: According to Wise, how do government officials justify secrecy? Does Wise think this is an acceptable justification?)**

---

11. Franz Boas, *The Mind of Primitive Man* (New York: Collier, 1911), 67.

12. R. D. Laing, *The Politics of Experience* (New York: Random House, 1967), 88–89. Copyright © R. D. Laing, 1967. Reprinted with permission of Penguin Books Ltd.

13. David Wise, *The Politics of Lying: Government, Deception, Secrecy, and Power* (New York: Random House, 1973), 501. Reprinted with permission of the publisher.

Finding an Argument
in a Sea of Words

In the previous section we concentrated on shortening passages to clarify meaning. Although such paraphrasing is helpful as a first step in understanding a variety of prose materials, our primary concern is illuminating arguments embedded in complex passages. They are the focus of the remainder of this chapter.

Often, only a small fraction of a passage actually conveys an argument. The remainder may consist of material designed to make the audience sympathetic with the position taken, statements intended to clarify the position, support for premises, and so forth.

Example 3.11 illustrates the problem you face when you try to apply techniques of reconstruction to more complicated passages. It is a short selection consisting of eight sentences (marked S1, S2, and so on) of the kind you might find in a newspaper.

Example 3.11

Activists Pit Civil Rights Against First Amendment

S1→ *Women activists have developed a new strategy in their fight against pornography. They are seeking to use civil rights laws to* ←S2 *attack what they consider exploitation of women that is promoted by pornographic materials.*

S3→ *In Minneapolis, Minnesota, these women successfully shepherded a measure through the City Council that would have opened the door for court action against any purveyor of films, magazines, or books that explicitly depict the sexual exploitation of women. Although the mayor ultimately vetoed the pro-* ←S4 *posed ordinance, the movement in Minneapolis and elsewhere in the country is growing as a result of impetus from both the feminist movement on the left and a new, public concern with morality on the right.*

S5→ *Opponents argue that the definition of pornography implicit in such laws is a grave threat to First Amendment rights of free expression. These critics point out that ironically enough such* ←S6 *ordinances could eliminate so-called Harlequin Romances that are widely purchased by women.*

S7→ *The conflict between these two positions is likely to remain unresolved until the U.S. Supreme Court rules on the constitutionality of provisions such as those in the Minneapolis ordinance. Another such case is brewing in Indiana.* ←S8

Although a headline is provided and the word *argue* is actually included in S5, it is not immediately obvious what argument is being presented or, indeed, whether any argument is being put forward. Many of the sentences (for example, S1, S2, S3, and S8) set the scene by offering a *description* of a state of affairs. Sentence 4 provides some description (namely, the mayor's veto), but it does something else as well: it offers an *explanation*[14] concerning why the movement is growing by pointing to support that extends across the political spectrum.

Sentences 5 and 6 present the most tempting candidates for a deductive argument. They would form the conclusion and premise of a valid argument with the addition of an implicit premise that any law that prohibits widely read books is a threat to First Amendment rights of free expression. But note that the author is not offering this argument herself. It is a *reported argument* from another source, which is not endorsed (or rejected) in the article. Finally S7, although it might seem like a conclusion, is not really argued for in the passage. No direct reasons are given for believing that the conflict will demand Supreme Court action. The statement is *unsupported in the context* of the passage. What about the headline? Is that a conclusion supported by the article? The passage itself describes a conflict in which one side appeals to civil rights and the other side appeals to the First Amendment. The headline is best construed as a *summary* of the overall content rather than as a conclusion for which reasons are offered.

This example illustrates several roles that statements can play other than as premises or conclusions in arguments. They can be:

descriptions

explanations

reports of arguments

statements unsupported in context

summaries

These are just some of the common tasks performed by sentences in typical passages that you are apt to come across in your search for arguments. We could add a few additional items also encountered frequently:

editorial comments

illustrations, examples, or classifications

analogies

---

14. The distinction between *explanation* and *argument* is discussed in chapter 10.

This list of roles statements can play should alert you to an important rule of thumb to guide you when you are looking for an argument in a piece of prose: *Much of what you find in prose passages is not part of an argument.*

Students in informal logic courses are often dismayed when they are asked to move beyond simplified classroom examples to essays, editorials, speeches, and other "real-world" passages. They read paragraph after paragraph without finding any arguments. But this should not be surprising when you consider how many roles a statement can play.

Seeing Argument Structure in Real-World Discourse   A useful first step when we are faced with a passage that contains much nonargument prose is to pick out the conclusion, find some statement or statements that seem to support the conclusion most directly, and then add whatever implicit premises are necessary. (Keep the argument patterns in mind.)

We can apply this method to the following passage:

Example 3.12

> *Well, I insist—and I here follow von Hildebrand—that we parents, we married people, in no way believe sex is dirty, but we believe it is private and intimate. Therefore, it cannot endure being publicized the way mathematics or even the way health is publicized. It is quite tactful for you to go to a party and talk about your tonsils. It is not tactful—not acceptable—for you to go to a party and talk about how your wife makes love to you, not because you think it is dirty, my friends, but because you think it is intimate.*[15]

In looking for the conclusion, the indicator word *therefore* directs our attention to the statement, "It [sex] cannot endure being publicized the way mathematics or even the way health is publicized." We can paraphrase what is essential here in a much simpler way:

Conclusion

> *Sex should not be publicized.*

Now we need to look through the passage to see what is offered as direct support for this conclusion. It is crucial to avoid simply listing all the sentences in the passage as though they were premises. Boil the passage down until it can be fit into a structured argument such as those represented by the patterns in chapters 2 and 4. In the first two lines, the author claims that she does not believe that sex is dirty. We can ignore this material for the purpose of reconstructing the argument, since we want to locate what she *does* believe in support of her conclusion. The second line

---

15. Quotation cited in Gloria Lentz, *Raping Our Children: The Sex Education Scandal* (New Rochelle, NY: Arlington House, 1972), 76.

presents a likely candidate, which we can write as a premise: *It (sex) is private and intimate*. So far, then, we have:

Example 3.13

(1) Sex is private and intimate.

∴ Sex should not be publicized.

Look at the remainder of the passage. It presents an example of something that may be publicized and claims again (in different words) that sex should not be publicized. None of this adds to the argument. What we need to get from the premise to the conclusion is a *general rule*. With a little thought you can see that the premise the passage leaves implicit is: Whatever is private and intimate should not be publicized. Adding this, we have:

Example 3.14

(implicit)

(1) Sex is private and intimate.

(2) Whatever is private and intimate should not be publicized.

∴ Sex should not be publicized.

For the purpose of reconstructing arguments, first approximations need not be written out in full. You may find it easier to penetrate the prose if you mark up the passage to indicate the central concepts (this might also involve noting whether the same concept is presented in different words). You can eliminate excess by simply crossing out irrelevant elements. And you can focus on argument structure by using some notation to check off "logical words" (such as *if . . . then, either . . . or, not, all,* and any indicator words). You can supplement these steps by identifying premises and conclusions. We have done this for the following passage, which offers a view of contemporary American culture.

Example 3.15

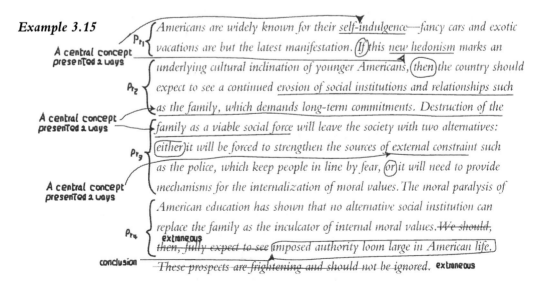

Once the passage has been analyzed in this way, it is easier to write out a sketch of the argument. This sketch might use just sentence fragments to display the main links. It is important to keep these elements relatively simple in the first stage of reconstruction so that you can easily understand the general "drift" of the argument.

Example 3.16   *Argument Sketch of the Passage About American Culture*

(1) Americans are self-indulgent.

(2) If self-indulgent, then erosion of values.

(3) If erosion of values, either internal or external constraint.

(4) No internal constraint.

∴ *External constraint.*

The reconstructions of Examples 3.12 and 3.15 illustrate how passages often demand extensive revision. In reconstructing an argument, as in paraphrasing single sentences, we have two conditions to meet: (1) the reconstruction should capture the apparent meaning of the original and (2) the reconstruction should provide more clarity. For any given argument, these guidelines can be satisfied by a number of different acceptable reconstructions.

Reconstructing Arguments with Subordinate Conclusions   Many passages contain several interrelated arguments. A reconstruction of such a passage may be presented in two different ways: (1) as several distinct arguments or (2) as a composite, continuous argument in which some statements are both a subordinate (or intermediate) conclusion and a premise.

Example 3.17   *(S1) A social policy promoting abortion will inevitably lead to greater violations of the rights of the person. (S2) Such a consequence will undermine the mutual respect for the humanity of fellow citizens upon which democratic society is based. (S3) Any policy that destroys social bonds in this way threatens the society that engages in it. (S4) Hence a social policy promoting abortion threatens democratic society.*

This passage can be reconstructed in two ways.

Reconstruction 1 (Two Separate Arguments)

(from S1) (Pr_1) *A social policy promoting abortion will inevitably lead to greater violations of the rights of the person.*

(rewrite of S2) (Pr_2) *A social policy that leads to greater violations of the rights of the person will undermine the mutual respect for the humanity of fellow citizens upon which democratic society is based.*

(implicit subordinate conclusion)   (C) ∴ *A social policy promoting abortion will inevitably undermine the mutual respect for the humanity of fellow citizens upon which democratic society is based.*

(conclusion from first argument) (C_1) *A social policy promoting abortion will inevitably undermine the mutual respect for the humanity of fellow citizens upon which democratic society is based.*

(rewrite of S3) (Pr_3) *Any policy that undermines the mutual respect for the humanity of fellow citizens upon which democratic society is based threatens the democratic society that practices it.*

(rewrite of S4)   (C) ∴ *A social policy promoting abortion will inevitably threaten the democratic society that practices it.*

Reconstruction 2 (as a Continuous Argument)

(Pr_1) *A social policy promoting abortion will inevitably lead to greater violations of the rights of the person.*

(Pr_2) *A social policy that leads to greater violations of the rights of the person will undermine the mutual respect for the humanity of fellow citizens upon which democratic society is based.*

(subordinate conclusion)   (C) ∴ *A social policy promoting abortion will inevitably undermine the mutual respect for the humanity of fellow citizens upon which democratic society is based.*

(Pr_3) *Any policy that undermines the mutual respect for the humanity of fellow citizens upon which democratic society is based threatens the democratic society that practices it.*

(main conclusion)   (C) ∴ *A social policy promoting abortion will inevitably threaten the democratic society that practices it.*

Whenever we strive to simplify or rewrite what someone else has produced, we run the risk of distorting what that writer said. The method of first approximation is a crude instrument designed to make rough cuts. Once we have discovered the basic structure, we can go back and paraphrase the argument more sensitively, thus capturing some of the subtleties we might have previously ignored. It is too easy for us to be lost in a sea of words when we face a complex passage. Simplification, paraphrase, and argument sketches are ways of finding our way through it.

Exercise 3.3   **Putting All This into Practice**

---

1. Reconstruct the arguments contained in the following passages. Simplify or paraphrase whenever possible. Add implicit conclusions or premises, or both, as needed. Most of the arguments can be reconstructed in several different ways.

   a. We can't restore democracy to Haiti. We can't restore democracy when it never existed.[16]

   b. I recognize, as do Roman Catholics generally, the great potential for human therapeutics in stem cell research. I do not oppose stem cell research per se if the cells are obtained from sources such as adult humans, miscarriages, or placental blood. What is morally unsustainable is the harvesting of stem cells by either of two currently proposed methods: (1) the creation and destruction of human embryos at the blastocyst stage by removal of the inner cell mass or (2) the harvesting of primordial germ cells from aborted fetuses. Both cases involve complicity in the direct interruption of a human life, which Roman Catholics believe has a moral claim to protection from the first moments of conception. In both cases, a living member of the human species is intentionally terminated.[17]

   c. Well, I insist—and I here follow von Hildebrand—that we parents, we married people, in no way believe sex is dirty, but we believe it is private and intimate. Therefore, it cannot endure being publicized the way mathematics or even the way health is publicized. It is quite tactful for you to go to a party and talk about your tonsils. It is not tactful—not acceptable— for you to go to a party and talk about how your wife makes love to you, not because you think it is dirty, my friends, but because you think it is intimate.[18] **(Hint: Go beyond the analysis given in the text. Treat this as an argument against sex education classes in the schools.)**

   d. There is a continuity of development from the moment of conception on. There are constant changes in the foetal condition; the foetus is constantly acquiring new structures and characteristics, but there is no one stage which is radically different from any other. Since that is so, there is no one stage in the process of foetal development, after the moment of conception, which could plausibly be picked out as the moment at which the foetus becomes a living human being. The moment of conception is, however,

---

16. CBS Sunday Evening News, July 17, 1994.

17. From Testimony of Edmund D. Pellegrino, M.D., before the National Bioethics Advisory Commission, published in *Ethical Issues in Human Stem Cell Research, Vol. III, Religious Perspectives,* Rockville, MD: June 2000.

18. Cited in Gloria Lentz, *Raping Our Children: The Sex Education Scandal* (New Rochelle, NY: Arlington House, 1972), 76.

different in this respect. It marks the beginning of this continuous process of development and introduces something new which is radically discontinuous with what has come before it. Therefore, the moment of conception, and only it, is a plausible candidate for being that moment at which the foetus becomes a living human being.[19] **(Hint: Try using the implicit premise that either the fetus becomes human at the moment of conception or it becomes human at some moment thereafter.)**

e. African-Americans have been subject to centuries of racism. Today, some blame the victims for the problems of our country. Don't they know that most African-Americans are hardworking, good citizens? . . . That important parts of American culture—from music to language to literature to fashion—have been created by African-Americans. I insist: All collective judgments are wrong. Only racists make them. And racism is stupid, just as it is ugly. Its aim is to destroy, to pervert, to distort innocence in human beings and their quest for human equality.[20]

f. A.L.T. Allen has been thinking about inner-city crime and violence and family deterioration. She's read the politicians, the sociologists and the pundits. And she thinks everybody has it wrong. ". . . The emphasis has been on the African-American male"—as the missing father and as the perpetrator and victim of violence. Says Allen: "It occurs to me that perhaps we are focusing on the wrong group. Our efforts should be aimed at reaching not the males, but the females. . . As long as women tolerate this behavior in men, it will continue. As long as women continue to have relationships with, and continue to bear the children of, men who do not marry them, men will continue to be absent fathers.[21]

g. Urban social programs can produce results, often enough to justify their costs. But none has shown a large impact on poverty. None can emancipate poor individuals and families from the personal problems of early pregnancy, crime and social failure that shackle them. . . . Choice or privatization can often improve the effectiveness of programs, but "empowerment" as a basis for anti-poverty policy tends to presume exactly what is questionable—the poor can be competent managers of their own lives. If poor adults behaved rationally they would seldom be poor for long in the first place. Opportunity is more available than the will to seize it. . . . The effect of racial bias is mainly to limit the quality of jobs blacks can get, not to deny them employment. . . . Without a "smoking gun," America

---

19. Baruch Brody, "On the Humanity of the Foetus," *Abortion: Pro and Con,* ed. Robert Perkins (Cambridge, MA: Shenkman, 1974), 70–71.
20. Elie Wiesel, "Have You Learned the Most Important Lesson of All?" *Parade Magazine,* 24 May 1992, 5. Elie Wiesel is a Nobel Peace Prize recipient.
21. William Raspberry, "Hope for a Decent Society May Lie with Young Women," *The Oregonian,* 30 November 1993, B5. William Raspberry is a syndicated columnist for the *Washington Post.*

cannot cure poverty with traditional reformism of either the left or right. Merely to expand government spending on the poor, or to cut it back does not motivate the entrenched poor to take available jobs. That is why neither the Great Society nor the Reagan era succeeded in overcoming poverty. Instead the nation needs a more authoritative social policy in which the needy are told how to live instead of merely being subsidized.[22]

h. If reporters want to get at the truth, they cannot continue to act as if only one side in this debate [over passive smoking] has an ax to grind. They need to be just as skeptical about the EPA and the Coalition on Smoking or Health as they are about Philip Morris. . . . Writing in *Toxicologic Pathology,* Yale epidemiologist Alvan Einstein cautioned his fellow scientists against automatically believing everything the "good guys" say and rejecting everything the "bad guys" say. His message applies to journalists as well as scientists: "If public health and epidemiology want to avoid becoming a branch of politics rather than science, the key issues are methods and process, not the 'goodness' of the goals or investigators. In science more than law, the 'bad guy' . . . should always have the right to state his case, and a well stated case has the right to be heard, regardless of who pays for it."[23]

i. So how should we react when the Philip Morris and R. J. Reynolds tobacco companies embark on an advertising campaign to convince us that second-hand smoke is harmless? . . . Who's telling the truth? Put the question to a simple test: who benefits and how? The tobacco giants have demonstrated that their paramount interest is protecting their $45 billion industry, and that the addiction, disease and premature death caused by cigarettes are not factors that concern them.[24]

j. Books and magazines that use a vocabulary that deludes women into thinking themselves rebels and outlaws, on the cusp of some new freedom, misperceive our basic situation. A defect in the early thinking of the women's movement was a tendency to liberate women not for life but for life in the counterculture; when that life was over, many women found themselves in limbo. . . . If we wish to be firm-voiced and progressive about meeting our primary needs, we should not point our heads in the direction of the wrong revolution. Vague definitions such as sister, rebel and outlaw may be handy for magazines in search of a vast circulation, but are of no use to thinking adults. Sexual liberation without economic security grants women merely the right to stay marginal. Women must cease being conned into substituting fantasy

22. Lawrence M. Mead, "Job Programs and Other Bromides," *New York Times* Op-Ed page, 19 May 1992, A19.

23. Jacob Sullum, "Passive Reporting on Passive Smoke," *Forbes MediaCritic.* From the last of a four-part series of advertisements titled "How to Spot Flaws in Secondhand Smoke Stories."

24. Gerald Alfers, *Olympian* (Olympia, WA), 18 July 1994, A7. Gerald Alfers is a board member and former president of the American Lung Association of Washington. His column was in response to the advertisement from which the previous passage was taken.

sexual revolutions for political pressure or real reforms that would give us true equality.[25]

2. The following selections each contain arguments. Use the techniques of reconstruction discussed in this chapter to reconstruct one or two of the more important and interesting ones.

a. *Lecture Fragment*

Plea bargaining (agreeing to plead guilty in exchange for a reduced sentence) generates problems. Innocent defendants who can't afford bail may plead guilty just to avoid jail time waiting for trial. The process makes no presumption of innocence. Guilt is not determined in an adversarial process, it is negotiated. It makes work easier for prosecutors, defense attorneys, and judges, but it sacrifices the interests of society.

Given these problems, some have suggested that plea bargaining be eliminated. But this might create an even worse problem. Ninety percent of defendants plead guilty, and most of those do plea-bargain.

Suppose plea bargaining were eliminated and the percentage of guilty pleas dropped to 80 percent. This would double the number of criminal trials, placing a staggering burden on the criminal justice system.

The experience of Alaska, however, calls this fear into question. Alaska has virtually done away with plea bargaining. There was some increase in the number of trials, but not as much as expected. In the year before elimination of plea bargaining, there were seventy-two felony trials in Fairbanks. In the year after, there were ninety. This is only a 25 percent increase.

Why was the increase so small? The explanation of why defendants plead guilty could be because most of them are factually guilty, and they don't have a viable legal argument for their defense (that is, they are legally guilty as well), so they believe it is unlikely they would win in a trial. If this is the case, then as Alaska's experience indicates, while it may be difficult to eliminate plea bargaining, it is not impossible.

(Note: There are several arguments in this lecture fragment. After formulating your reconstructions, compare them to those made on page 10. Remember that the reconstruction of arguments from longer passages allows for some degree of individual interpretation.)

---

25. Barbara Probst Solomon, "This Take-a-Lover Chatter Overlooks the Bottom Line," *International Herald Tribune*, 10 July 1992, 7.

b.

License Users of Guns, Just Like Drivers of Cars
Opposing view: Only the law-abiding will submit to such restrictions, thereby making crime easier
(By André Marrou, 1992 Libertarian Party presidential nominee)[26]

If anti-gun laws worked, then New York and Washington, with the toughest anti-gun laws, would have the lowest crime rates. But they have the *highest*.

Conversely, crime rates plummeted up to 90% after certain cities and states—like Orlando, Fla., and Kennesaw, Ga.—allowed law-abiding citizens to carry concealed handguns.

The reason should be obvious: law-abiding citizens know and obey the law. Criminals don't care what the law is and won't obey it. So who benefits when gun ownership and use are restricted? The criminals, because decent folks are disarmed by the law, making it easier for criminals to prey upon them.

Registering guns and licensing gun owners won't reduce crime any more than registering cars and licensing drivers now reduce traffic accidents—which is to say, hardly at all. With millions of highly restrictive laws, still about 44,000 Americans yearly die in traffic accidents, while about 15,000 are shot to death. Since there are fewer cars than guns, cars are clearly more dangerous than guns. Should we outlaw cars?

Like cars, guns are dangerous tools. So are kitchen knives (ask John Bobbitt) and chain saws; should we register or outlaw them, or license their use? Just because something is dangerous—say climbing mountains or riding bulls—doesn't mean we should restrict its use or test and license its practitioners.

Guns are tools, not evil instruments capable of their own malevolence. A gun simply amplifies its user's power. In a rapist's hands, a gun is bad; in a law-abiding woman's hand, it's good. New York and Washington have proved that guns cannot be kept from criminal hands; shouldn't we let decent people arm themselves without licensing?

Ultimately, "gun control" is not about guns. It's about control. Beware.

---

26. The January 1, 1994, issue of *USA TODAY* contained an editorial titled "License Users of Guns, Just Like Drivers of Cars," which presented the position of the editorial staff. It defended the position that "as a matter of public safety and accountability, the states should require that all gun users be licensed." The André Marrou selection above presents an opposing view.

c.

The First Amendment Unworthily Used[27]

A lawyer for the Brooklyn Museum of Art misappropriated a revered American concept in a hearing stemming from the museum's controversial art exhibit.

The laywer was protesting an order by New York City Mayor Rudolph Giuliani to deny the museum $7.2 million in city financing in retaliation for its showing of the exhibit, which included a portrait of the Virgin Mary partly composed of elephant feces and surrounded by pornographic cutouts. Catholic groups have called the portrait offensive.

Denial of the museum funds, the lawyer said, is a First Amendment catastrophe. He likened it to a book burning, the destruction of free expression. The First Amendment prohibits Congress from abridging the freedom of speech.

Certainly Giuliani's fund-withholding tactic leaves plenty of room for criticism. As has been said before in this space, the ideal relationship between the government and the arts is a hands-off policy, even if the government is paying part of the bill. Otherwise, the result is to have elected officials or bureaucrats deciding what is or isn't art, an assignment that they are rarely qualified to carry out.

Of course, the arts professionals to whom the responsibility is delegated also have a responsibility to exercise judgment. More than once in recent years, people in such a position have seemed to let their judgment be guided mostly by considerations of what would shock and offend—stuff that, as has been noted in some cases, would constitute a hate crime if it were smeared on the wall of a church or synagogue instead of being hung in a museum.

Giuliani is entitled to criticize the exhibit. But the directors of the museum were hired to exercise judgment. Just because the mayor disagrees with their judgment is insufficient cause to nuke their funding for the year. His are the actions of a man who has lost perspective.

---

27. Copyright 1999 by the *Omaha World-Herald*. Reprinted with permission.

The same is true of the lawyer. The city has suppressed nothing. No paintings have been banned or burned. No one has been barred by law from seeing the exhibit.

Indeed, it is widely predicted that the controversy has raised the potential market price of items in the display, some of which may be put up for sale when the run at the Brooklyn is finished.

The only question involved here is whether offensive art has an unquestioned entitlement to public subsidy. To make that a first Amendment question is a misrepresentation. The owner of the art is free to display it around the country and to assume he will have the backing of the courts if the government tries to stop him.

 CHAPTER FOUR

Evaluating Arguments: Some Basic Questions

This chapter will focus on two questions we must ask when we evaluate an argument:

1. Does the conclusion follow from the premises?

2. Should the premises be accepted as true?

If the conclusion does follow and the premises are true, then we call an argument sound. Corresponding to these two criteria of soundness are two ways of criticizing an argument: showing that the conclusion does not follow and showing that the premises are doubtful (Table 4.1).

Table 4.1

Criteria for Soundness	*Corresponding Criticisms*
1. Conclusion follows from premises	1. Show that conclusion doesn't follow from the premises
2. Premises are true	2. Show that premises are doubtful

Before we explore these two features that we look for in a good argument and the corresponding criticisms we can make of bad arguments, it will be helpful to explain the difference between them. Obviously, Examples 4.1 and 4.2 are both faulty arguments, but what is wrong with 4.1 is wholly different from what is wrong with 4.2.

Example 4.1

(1) If AIDS is harmless, then we need not take precautions against it.

(2) AIDS is harmless.

∴ We need not take precautions against AIDS.

Conclusion follows but premise 2 is false

Example 4.2

(1) Any disease that threatens many lives is worth our concern.

(2) Mumps is worth our concern.

∴ Mumps is a disease that threatens many lives.

Premises are true but conclusion does not follow

When we say that the conclusion does not follow from the premises, as in Example 4.2, we are saying that something is wrong with the *form* or *pattern* of the argument. On the other hand, when we say that a premise is not acceptable, as in Example 4.1, it is the content, not the pattern of the argument, that we are criticizing.

Think of an argument as like a building, with the premises being the foundation, the conclusion being the house that it supports, and the form or pattern of the argument being the design of the building. The design could be a perfectly good one, but if the foundation is made of weak material the house could collapse. Similarly, an argument could fit a correct pattern, but if the premises are false, the conclusion could be false as well. On the other hand, the foundation could be perfectly strong, but if the design is faulty, the house might collapse in this case too because of this poor design. Analogously, an argument could have true premises but an incorrect pattern, in which case the conclusion could be false. Example 4.1 is like a building with a good design but a faulty foundation. The pattern is *modus ponens* from our list of common successful patterns, but the second premise—*AIDS is harmless*—is obviously false. Example 4.2 is like a building with a strong foundation (true premises) but a bad design.

Pattern of Example 4.2 (Faulty Argument)

(1) All P_1's are P_2's.

(2) m is a P_2.

∴ m is a P_1.

The following section will explain some ways of showing that for any argument with this pattern, the conclusion does not follow from the premises.

In contrast to Examples 4.1 and 4.2, Example 4.3 both exhibits one of the common successful patterns from our list and in addition has true premises. Logicians call this property *soundness*: having true premises and a conclusion that follows from them (a good foundation and a good structural fit).

Example 4.3   ***Sound argument: True premises from which the conclusion follows***

(1) Any disease that threatens many lives is worth our concern.

(2) AIDS threatens many lives.

∴ *AIDS is worth our concern.*

Again, an argument's conclusion follows from its premises because of the form, or pattern, of the argument. The technical term for this property of having a correct pattern so that the conclusion does indeed follow is *validity*. Validity plus true premises constitutes soundness.

In the following section, we discuss in greater detail what it means for the conclusion to follow from the premises and offer some techniques for showing that the conclusion does not follow. This topic of how to determine the validity or invalidity of an argument is treated more formally in the next (optional) chapter of the book.

When Does the Conclusion Follow from the Premises?

In chapter 2 we presented a chart of seven argument patterns. A portion of this chart is repeated below. We claimed that, for any argument that fits one of these patterns, its conclusion follows from its premise.

Some Common Successful Argument Patterns

i. *Modus Ponens*	**ii. *Disjunctive Argument***	**iii. *Modus Tollens***
(1) If A, then B.	*(1) Either A or B.*	*(1) If A, then B.*
(2) A.	*(2) Not A.*	*(2) Not B.*
∴ *B.*	∴ *B.*	∴ *Not A.*

iv. *Hypothetical Argument*	**v. *Chain Argument***
(1) If A, then B.	*(1) A.*
(2) If B, then C.	*(2) If A, then B*
∴ *If A, then C.*	*(3) If B, then C.*
	∴ *C.*

vi. *Predicate Instantiation*	**vii. *Universal Syllogism***
(1) All P_1's are P_2's.	*(1) All P_1's are P_2's.*
(2) m is a P_1.	*(2) All P_2's are P_3's.*
∴ *m is a P_2.*	∴ *All P_1's are P_3's.*

What do we mean when we say that the conclusion of an argument follows from its premises? A less metaphorical way of putting it is that if the premises are true, then the conclusion must necessarily be true. In other words, it is impossible for the premises to be true and the conclusion false. We will try to make this clearer by contrasting several of the successful patterns from the chart with unsuccessful ones—patterns that would permit the possibility that the premises could be true but the conclusion false. At the same time, we will illustrate two techniques of showing that a conclusion doesn't follow from the premises. Two sentence-based patterns from the chart, *modus ponens* and *modus tollens,* were contrasted to unsuccessful patterns in chapter 2. Here we will examine the predicate-based patterns.

Example 4.4

Successful Pattern	*Contrasting Unsuccessful Pattern*
vii. Universal Syllogism	
(1) All P_1's are P_2's.	*(1) All P_1's are P_2's.*
(2) All P_2's are P_3's.	*(2) All P_2's are P_3's.*
∴ All P_1's are P_3's.	*∴ All P_3's are P_1's.*

For any argument that fits the pattern on the left, if the premises are true, then the conclusion must be true. An argument could fit the pattern on the right, however, and have true premises and a false conclusion. Here is an example of each kind of argument.

Example 4.5

Argument A	*Argument B (Faulty)*
(1) All good teachers treat students with respect.	*(1) All good teachers treat students with respect.*
(2) All who treat students with respect listen to what students say.	*(2) All who treat students with respect listen to what students say.*
∴ All good teachers listen to what students say.	*∴ All who listen to what students say are good teachers.*

When we say that the conclusion of argument A follows from its premises (that is, that the argument is valid), we are making a universal claim about all arguments that fit this same pattern. We are saying that the pattern is such that it will always take us from true premises to a true conclusion. Make up any argument you like. As long as the premises are true and they fit the pattern:

(1) All P_1's are P_2's.

(2) All P_2's are P_3's.

then the conclusion, *All P_1's are P_3's*, will be true also. For example, it is true that *all cats are mammals* and *all mammals are animals*. Since these premises fit the stated pattern, it follows that *all cats are animals*.

How do we evaluate whether an argument's conclusion follows from the premises? Our list of successful argument patterns provides a method for *some* cases. As we indicated in chapter 2, any argument fitting these patterns is valid, that is, the premises follow from the conclusion. But what should a practitioner of critical reasoning do if the argument in question does not fit one of these patterns? The techniques of formal logical allow us to assess the validity of the arguments more broadly—we discuss some of them in chapter 5—but there are also two informal techniques that can be used for showing invalidity: finding a counterexample and explaining how the premises could be true and the conclusion false.

The Counterexample Method of Showing That an Argument's Conclusion Does Not Follow   Since the claim that an argument's conclusion follows from its premises is universal (it applies to *all* cases having the same pattern), we can identify one way of showing that an argument's conclusion does not follow—that is, give a counterexample to this general claim.[1] The general claim (which is implicit any time we advance an argument) is: *all arguments that fit this same pattern and have true premises will have a true conclusion*. A counterexample to this claim, then, is an argument that *fits the same pattern*, has (obviously) *true premises*, and has an (obviously) *false conclusion*.

Suppose someone actually advanced Example 4.5, argument B:

(1) All good teachers treat students with respect.

(2) All who treat students with respect listen to what students say.

∴ *All who listen to what students say are good teachers.*

The person who advances this argument, in believing that the conclusion follows from the premises, is implicitly committed to the belief that if any other argument fits this same pattern, its conclusion will also follow from its premises. To give a

---

1. The counterexample method of showing that an argument pattern is invalid should not be confused with the counterexample method of showing that a universal premise is false. The latter is explained on page 94.

counterexample, then, we could say: "That's just like arguing: '*All cats are mammals, and all mammals are animals, so all animals are cats'!*" This argument fits the same pattern as argument B and the premises are obviously true, but the conclusion is obviously false.

Method 1: Find a Counterexample

To show that the conclusion of an argument does not follow from the premises, you should:

1. Determine the pattern of the argument you wish to criticize,

2. Make up a new argument, with
   a. the same pattern,
   b. obviously true premises, and
   c. an obviously false conclusion.

We say "obviously true" premise and "obviously false" conclusion because you want to make it as clear as possible to the arguer (and to yourself) that the pattern in question can take you from true premises to a false conclusion. It is a good idea to use simple, familiar objects and relationships in your counterexample, as we did in the argument about cats, mammals, and animals.

This counterexample method is the main one we recommend for criticizing the structure of arguments in ordinary discourse. Even this simple method requires an audience willing to listen patiently and thoughtfully to understand your point. More sophisticated techniques might not be readily understood except by those already schooled in logic. For a general audience, you might have even avoided referring to arguments with correct patterns as *valid,* because this technical logician's term could be misleading. Since many people would think of a valid argument as completely successful, not just formally correct, it would be confusing to them to hear an argument referred to as valid if it had obviously false premises.

The other predicate-based pattern on our list can also be contrasted to a similar but unsuccessful version:

Example 4.6

Successful Pattern	*Contrasting Unsuccessful Pattern*
vi. Predicate Instantiation	
(1) All P_1's are P_2's.	*(1) All P_1's are P_2's.*
(2) m is a P_1.	*(2) m is a P_2.*
∴ *m is a P_2.*	∴ *m is a P_1.*

Because argument A, below, fits the successful pattern, its conclusion follows from its premises, while for argument B (which fits the unsuccessful pattern), the conclusion does not follow.

Example 4.7

Argument A	Argument B (Faulty)
(1) All good athletes are well coordinated.	(1) All good athletes are well coordinated.
(2) Mario is a good athlete.	(2) Mario is well coordinated.
∴ Mario is well coordinated.	∴ Mario is a good athlete.

Because of its successful pattern, it is impossible for the premises of argument A to be true and its conclusion to be false. This is not to say that the argument's premises or its conclusion are in fact true—Mario could be a terrible athlete and poorly coordinated. But as long as the premises *are true,* the conclusion will be true also. Furthermore, for any other argument that fits this pattern, if it has true premises, it will also have a true conclusion. In this section, we do not discuss techniques for showing that an argument has a successful pattern (this is done in chapter 5), but a few moments' thought should assure you that the pattern of argument A in Example 4.7 will always take you from true premises to a true conclusion. The first premise asserts that one class of things is contained in a second class of things. The second premise locates a certain individual in the first class. Now if this first class is contained in the second class of things, the individual (Mario in this case) can't be in the first class without being in the second class. What the argument asserts is true no matter what classes and what individuals we are discussing. A second example of this successful pattern would be:

Argument with Same Pattern as Example 4.7A

Argument A

All U.S. presidents have been U.S. citizens.

Clinton has been a U.S. president.

∴ Clinton has been a U.S. citizen.

Using these same familiar relationships, we can construct a counterexample to show that the conclusion of argument B does not follow from its premises:

Counter-example to Example 4.7B

Argument B

(1) All U.S. presidents have been U.S. citizens.

(2) I have been a U.S. citizen.

∴ I have been a U.S. president.

Since this argument has true premises and a false conclusion and fits the same pattern as argument B, the pattern of argument B is not successful: argument B's conclusion does not follow from its premises.

A Second Method of Showing That an Argument's Conclusion Does Not Follow   Although this counterexample method is often the easiest way to show that a conclusion doesn't follow, a second method is sometimes easier yet: we can simply explain how it would be possible for the premises of an argument to be true but the conclusion false. This doesn't involve making up a new argument, just discussing the argument at hand. Again, we can use argument B as an example:

Example 4.7B   **Argument B**

All good athletes are well coordinated.

Mario is well coordinated.

∴ *Mario is a good athlete.*

The following passage describes a possible situation in which the premises of argument B are true and the conclusion is false:

> *Suppose it is true that all good athletes are well coordinated and that Mario has excellent coordination. But suppose also that Mario is extremely slow, in bad physical condition, and has never practiced any athletic endeavors.*

Here we have a situation in which the premises of argument B would be true but the conclusion is false. But what it means for the conclusion of an argument to follow from the premises is that it is impossible for the premises to be true and the conclusion false. Hence, we have shown that the conclusion of argument B does not follow from the premises.

Method 2: Describe an Invalidating Possible Situation

To show that the conclusion of an argument *does not follow* from the premises, you should:

> Describe a possible situation in which the premises are obviously true and the conclusion is obviously false.

Consider the following argument:

Example 4.8   **Argument to Be Evaluated**

(1) *If alcohol consumption is declining, then drunken driving is declining.*

(2) *If drunken driving is declining, then the auto accident rate is declining.*

(3) *The auto accident rate is declining.*

∴ *Alcohol consumption is declining.*

This argument has the pattern:[2]

> *(1) If A, then B.*
>
> *(2) If B, then C.*
>
> *(3) C.* _____
>
> ∴ *A.*

We can see this is an invalid argument by using either of the two methods described above. By method 1, we can construct a counterexample.

Example 4.9

Counterexample

> *(1) If the White House is in Cleveland, then it is in Ohio.*
>
> *(2) If the White House is in Ohio, then it is in the United States.*
>
> *(3) The White House is in the United States.* _____
>
> ∴ *The White House is in Cleveland.*

All three of the premises are true. If any building is in Cleveland, then it is in Ohio. If a building is in Ohio, then it is in the United States. Finally, the White House is in the United States. But of course, it is in Washington, D.C., not in Cleveland, Ohio. This counterexample shows that the original argument does not reflect a valid argument form.

Method 2 leads us to describe a situation in which the argument to be evaluated has true premises and a false conclusion. Suppose that highways are improved or the proportion of young male drivers declines. Each of these could produce a decrease in the accident rate, even though the amount of alcohol consumption does not decline. In such a case all the premises could be true and the conclusion false.

Both these methods focus on showing that it is possible for all the premises to be true and the conclusion false. When a deductive argument is valid, it is *impossible* for this to occur. This logical impossibility is due to the form or pattern of the argument. We discuss logical impossibility at greater length in chapter 5. For now, a few physical analogies should help introduce the concept.

> An argument is valid just in case there is no possible situation in which all of its premises are true and its conclusion is false.

---

2. This should not be mistaken for the valid argument form

> *(1) If A, then B.*
>
> *(2) If B, then C.*
>
> *(3) A.* _____
>
> ∴ *C.*

which is a variant of pattern (v) on our chart.

Depicting Validity   An analogy with physical impossibility is useful in clarifying the concept of validity for statement-based arguments. It illustrates a connection between structure (in this case physical structure) and possibility. As shown below, we can model the valid chain argument by representing premises 1 and 2 as an arrangement of blocks or dominoes set up close to each other. If the first is pushed, then the others fall in turn, until the last (C) falls as well. In this model, it is impossible to push A without C falling, given how the blocks are related to each other. The same is true for the logical links created by the if-then statements. If A is true, then C must be as well.

Valid Argument Pattern

(1) If A, then B.

(2) If B, then C.

(3) A.

∴ *C.*

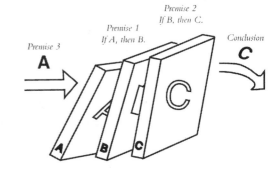

Contrast this relation with that of the invalid argument actually found in the example:

Invalid Argument Pattern

(1) If A, then B.

(2) If B, then C.

(3) C.

∴ *A.*

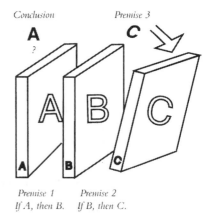

In this case, pushing block C doesn't force A to fall, even though A is next to B and B is next to C. Similarly, as the application of the two methods shows, it is logically possible for the premises to be true and the conclusion false.

The analogy with falling blocks is not meant as a method for testing validity. Another way of depicting validity is also a method of testing validity for some arguments. Simple examples of predicate-based arguments can be represented using Venn diagrams.[3] Consider the following valid "predicate-based" argument from Example 4.7A.

Argument: Example 4.7A	*Pattern: Predicate Instantiation*
(1) All good athletes are well coordinated.	*(1) All P_1's are P_2's.*
(2) Mario is a good athlete.	*(2) m is a P_1.*
∴ *Mario is well coordinated.*	∴ *m is a P_2.*

Unlike statement-based arguments, which depend on the relationship of statements joined by connecting words such as *if-then* and *either-or*, predicate-based arguments depend on the internal structure of statements. We can illustrate the structure of a statement like *All good athletes are well coordinated*—which exhibits the pattern "All P_1's are P_2's"—using the following Venn diagram:

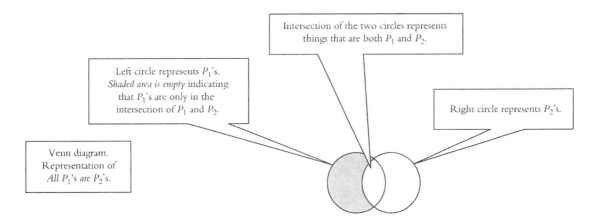

Intersection of the two circles represents things that are both P_1 and P_2.

Left circle represents P_1's. *Shaded area is empty* indicating that P_1's are only in the intersection of P_1 and P_2.

Right circle represents P_2's.

Venn diagram. Representation of All P_1's are P_2's.

The left-hand circle represents the class of P_1's (in this case, good athletes), and the right-hand circle represents the class of P_2's (in this case, the well coordinated). By shading the part of the P_1's circle that doesn't overlap the P_2's circle, we are indicating that this part of the circle is *empty*—that all P_1's are P_2's. Now if we place an *m* in the unshaded part of the P_1's circle, indicating that *m* is a P_1 (in our argument,

---

3. Named after British logician John Venn (1834–1923), who developed this method of presenting relationships.

Mario is a good athlete), we see that *m* *must* lie within the P_2's circle, which is our conclusion—*m* is a P_2 (Mario is well coordinated) according to pattern (vi) for Predicate Instantiation.

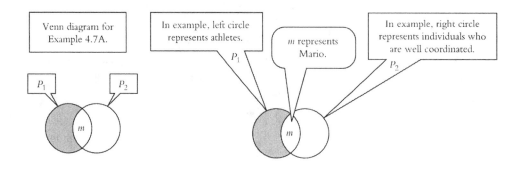

This diagram shows that the argument is valid by showing that the only possible situation that makes the premises true also makes the conclusion true. If it is true that all P_1's are P_2's (*All althletes are well coordinated*), then we must represent the portion of the P_1 circle that is outside the P_2 circle as being empty—it is an impossible situation for premise 1 to be true and for some P_1 to not be a P_2. If premise 2 is also true, then we are compelled to put *m* (Mario) in the unshaded part of the P_1 circle. We can't represent him as being outside the P_1 circle since premise 2 says he is a P_1. The only place left to put him is in the part of the P_1 circle that is also inside the P_2 circle. But now we see that by representing the premises in the only way possible, we have already represented the conclusion: *m* is a P_2. It is impossible to put *m* outside the P_2 circle without making at least one of the premises false. This shows that the argument is valid.

These ways of making the conclusion false also make a premise false. There is no possible way of making both the premises true without making the conclusion true.

Premise 1 false

Premise 2 false

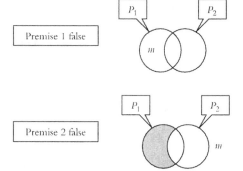

By contrast consider the invalid argument from Example 4.7B.

Argument: Example 4.7B	*Faulty Argument Pattern*
(1) All good athletes are well coordinated.	*(1) All P_1's are P_2's.*
(2) Mario is well coordinated.	*(2) m is a P_2.*
∴ *Mario is a good athlete.*	∴ *m is a P_1.*

We can represent a possible counterexample using the same circles and shading as before for the first premise, but this time we are not assured of the truth of the conclusion. As shown below, one possible way in which the second premise could be true is represented by the *m?* in the P_2 circle (indicating that Mario is well coordinated). In this case, the conclusion is false because *m* is not in the P_1 class (i.e., Mario is not a good athlete).[4]

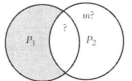

How Often Do We Need to Show That an Argument's Conclusion Doesn't Follow?

It is actually rare in everyday discourse to encounter an argument whose conclusion *clearly* doesn't follow from its premises. This is partly because it is rare for all the premises and the conclusion of an argument to be explicitly stated. If we make a charitable interpretation of what has been said or written, we can almost always reconstruct an argument so that its conclusion follows. However, it is still important to understand the concept of validity and to be able to explain to yourself why the conclusions of some arguments don't follow from the premises. In fact, whenever you reconstruct an argument with missing parts, you must think about correct structure as you attempt to make the argument fit a successful pattern. We might say that the criterion that the conclusion must follow from the premises is used primarily in *self-evaluating* your reconstruction of an argument rather than in expressing a criticism of someone else's argument.

---

4. Of course, *m* could also be in the intersection of P_1 and P_2 as represented by the *?*. But it *need not* be. If an argument is valid, then there is no possibility that the premises are all true and the conclusion is false. This Venn diagram depicts just such a situation. So the argument is invalid. Chapter 5 contains further discussion of Venn diagrams as a method of testing the validity of simple predicate-based argument patterns.

Notice that this section gives you some techniques for showing that an argument's conclusion *doesn't* follow, but no techniques for showing that a conclusion *does* follow. As we have said, in most cases when you reconstruct an argument you will either make it follow one of the seven successful patterns or a pattern that is such a simple variation or combination of these patterns that you can readily see that it is successful. Another reason is that the techniques for showing that a conclusion does follow require considerable explanation and some introduction of formal symbols, as we indicate in (optional) chapter 5.

Exercise 4.1   **Showing Invalidity**

Show that each of the following arguments is invalid (that is, the conclusion doesn't follow from the premises). Use either the counterexample method or the possible situation method. Explain what you are doing clearly enough that an intelligent general audience would understand the point you are making.

1. Anyone who lives with a smoker has an above-average risk of heart disease. Sarah doesn't live with a smoker. So Sarah doesn't have an above-average risk of heart disease.

2. If federal government oversight is lax, then corporate crime will increase. Corporate crime has increased. So federal government oversight is lax.

3. If dinner guests are coming, then we need more food. If we need more food, then we need to go to the store. Dinner guests aren't coming. Therefore, we don't need to go to the store.

4. No great singer has a weak voice. Kim is not a great singer. It follows that Kim has a weak voice.

5. If the American people feel overtaxed, then they will press for tax cuts. The American people don't feel overtaxed. So they won't press for tax cuts.

6. All doctors have studied medicine. Paul is not a doctor. Therefore, Paul has not studied medicine.

7. All compassionate people are honest people. This is so because all good friends are compassionate people, and all good friends are honest people.

8. Nanotechnology is the business opportunity of the future. This is so because stocks in technology will be strong. If nanotechnology is the business opportunity of the future, then it will attract more investment. If it will attract more investment, then stocks in technology will be strong.

9. Anyone who is good at science is good at math. Anyone who is good at math is intelligent. So, anyone who is intelligent is good at science.

10. Either we will ration health care, or we will spend too much on health care. We will ration health care. So we won't spend too much on health care. **(Hint: To call this argument invalid is to take the word *or* in the inclusive sense of "either A or B or both." A counterexample would need to be an argument of the same pattern that clearly used *or* in this inclusive sense.)**

When Should the Premises Be Accepted As True?

As we have seen, an argument's conclusion can follow from its premises, even though some or all of the premises are false.

Example 4.10

(1) If an effective cure for AIDS is available, the world community should provide it to all who need it but can't afford it.

(2) An effective cure for AIDS is available.

∴ *The world community should provide it to all who need it but can't afford it.*

Unfortunately, although this argument is valid (that is, its conclusion follows), the second premise is false. (At least we take it to be false at the time of the writing of this book.) Because the second premise is false, the argument is not sound; it doesn't justify our belief in the conclusion.

In general, the question of whether an argument's conclusion follows can be answered with greater certainty than the question of whether its premises are true. As we have noted, logicians have developed techniques that can tell us whether an argument is correctly structured, even when we are dealing with much more complex arguments than those illustrated on our list of patterns. By contrast, there is no general method of determining whether premises are true or false.

Most of the arguments we encounter in our everyday lives have premises whose truth or falsity cannot be determined with certainty. Consider our *judgment* that the argument about an AIDS cure (Example 4.10) is *unsound* because the premise *An effective cure for AIDS is available* is *false*. We are not as certain about this judgment of falsity as we would be if an argument contained statements from arithmetic. We can only give reasons why it is highly unlikely that an AIDS cure is available. For example, we can point out that this would be such important news that we surely would have heard about it, and that it would be difficult to suppress news of the discovery of an AIDS cure.

We use reasons such as these to justify our *judgment* that the premise *A cure for AIDS is available* is false even though we are not absolutely certain that it is false. And we use comparable reasons for making judgments that some premises of arguments are true. Sometimes we are relatively certain about premises because of clear, direct observations we have made (for example, that a friend has acted aggressively) or because we have evidence from many independent sources (for instance, that the U.S. deficit has increased). But at other times, we must decide whether to accept the premises of an argument when we are not all that certain of their truth or falsity.

Most of the examples and exercises in the remainder of the book are not ones in which you will be led to a clear, definite decision: "This argument is sound." You will sometimes be able to determine with absolute certainty that an argument is *unsound* because it is *invalid*—that is, the conclusion doesn't follow. But typically, you will be reconstructing the arguments you read in a way that makes them valid. Then the question remains of whether you should accept the premises as true. Answering this will be an exercise in using the background information and beliefs you already possess to give reasons for or against accepting premises.

Even though there is no general methodology for determining whether premises should be accepted as true, there are techniques that can be quite successful for criticizing certain broad categories of premises. Some of these are described in the following section.

Tips on Casting Doubt on Premises   Since any kind of statement can serve as a premise in an argument, the question of how to cast doubt on premises is obviously too broad to be dealt with here in detail. How can you cast doubt on any statement? We have to assume that this is the sort of thing you already know how to do. We can, however, provide some techniques for attacking certain kinds of premises, as well as advice concerning which kinds of premises can be criticized most easily and fruitfully. The techniques we introduce in this section are: (1) giving counterexamples to premises that generalize, (2) breaking the connection in if-then premises, and (3) scrutinizing further implications of premises.

Perhaps the most straightforward criticism of a premise is a counterexample to a universal generalization.[5] If a premise claims that *All P_1's are P_2's*, or that *No P_1's are P_2's*—*All lying is wrong; No sea animals are mammals*—try to think of a clear counterexample (lying to save an innocent person's life; whales or seals). Some universal generalizations are true, but many can be shown to be false by pointing out that something is clearly a P_1 but is clearly not a P_2. Or, if the claim is that *No P_1's are P_2's,* point to something that is *clearly* a P_1 and is clearly also a P_2. When we say "clearly," we mean that it should be uncontroversial to your audience that your counterexample really is a counterexample. Some additional examples will show why this is important.

---

5. A universal statement applies to every case (in the "universe" under discussion). In this case it says that everything has a characteristic *(All P_1's are P_2's)* or everything does not have the characteristic *(No P_1's are P_2's)*.

Suppose someone is arguing that all abortion should be illegal, and this person uses the premise *All killing of human beings is wrong.* You want to present as a counterexample something that is clearly a case of killing but that is clearly not wrong. To state that executing a murderer is not wrong would not be as effective for most audiences as to use the counterexample of killing another person in self-defense. This is because capital punishment is a controversial issue, and your audience might believe that executing a murderer is wrong. Then you would be sidetracked into debating this second issue. It is much less likely that your audience would believe that killing in self-defense is wrong, particularly if you described a situation in which killing the assailant was the only alternative to being killed. Obviously, the worst kind of attempted counterexample in this context would be to claim that killing a fetus is not wrong, since the issue being discussed is abortion and the arguer, presumably, believes that killing a fetus is wrong.

Consider the universal generalization: Any practice that is harmful should be illegal. Contrast the clear counterexamples below to the controversial or "borderline" counterexamples.

Any practice that is harmful should be illegal.

Good Counterexample	*Controversial, Borderline Counterexample*
Neglecting to exercise	Hang gliding
Eating many doughnuts	Russian roulette

Neglecting to exercise and eating many doughnuts are practices that are somewhat harmful to health, but surely they should not be illegal. The borderline cases are more controversial. Hang gliding and Russian roulette are clearly harmful, but some would claim that they should be illegal as well.

A second broad category of premise that can be challenged in a fairly straightforward way is an *if-then* premise, which claims a connection between two things. If the premise is of this type, try to think of ways the first thing could occur without the second occurring. For example, consider the premise *If birthrates continue to increase, then the world will become overcrowded.* What if death rates increase more rapidly than birthrates? What if people start colonizing other planets? In both cases, the first condition could occur—birthrate could continue to increase—without the second occurring—overcrowding of the world.

This kind of criticism is weaker than a clear counterexample to a universal generalization. Raising the possibility that the "if" part won't be followed by the "then" part doesn't show that the premise is false, just that it is less than certain. The more likely the event that would break the if-then connection, the less likely the premise.

A third kind of criticism can be attempted against any premise. That is, every premise has *further implications*—statements that *would* be true if the premise in question were true. Try to think of such implications, particularly ones that are highly doubtful. For example, someone might use as a premise the claim that punishment does not deter crime. This implies that if there were no punishment, there would still be no more crime than there is now. Do you believe this? For example, would you personally still refrain from stealing to the same extent that you do now, even if you knew you wouldn't be punished? Would you still pay your income taxes?

Some Ways to Cast Doubt on Premises

1. Presenting a counterexample for a universal generalization

2. Finding a clear case in which antecedent is true, consequent false for an if-then premise

3. For any premise, pointing out further implications that are doubtful

---

In general, after you have determined whether an argument's conclusion follows from its premises, you will want to survey the premises to decide where to begin your evaluation. As a general strategy, we suggest initially directing your attention to premises that can be discussed on the basis of generally shared background information. This is certainly preferable to quibbling over matters that require research and documentation that can't actually be carried out on the occasion of the discussion. Then, if you determine that your appraisal of the argument really hinges on specific facts that need to be researched, you can do the necessary investigation.

Much of the material in the following chapters will help you criticize more specialized kinds of premises. Chapter 6, on fallacies, will identify some specific kinds of premises that are typically doubtful. Chapter 7 will help you evaluate definition-like premises. Premises that make statistical generalizations based on observational data will be scrutinized in chapter 8. Sometimes, elements of scientific theories are used as premises. Techniques for evaluating such premises are discussed in chapter 10.

Exercise 4.2   **Casting Doubt on Premises**

Each of the following statements might occur as a premise in an argument. (Indeed, some of them are used as premises in the arguments in Exercise 4.4.) For each statement, think about what you might say to persuade someone that the claim being made is not true—or at least that it is doubtful. If you need more information about a topic, do a little research, either by consulting a source or by talking with someone you consider knowledgeable about the subject. Then put your ideas into writing, formulating a short paragraph casting doubt on each statement. Keep in mind the tips for casting doubt on universal claims and on if-then claims. If you find yourself initially inclined to agree with a statement, try to imagine what an intelligent critic on the other side of the issue might say to cast doubt on it.

1. If capital punishment is completely abolished, then the homicide rate will increase rapidly.

2. People shouldn't make promises unless they are certain they can keep them.

3. Any activity that makes people aggressive should be discouraged.

4. If the fetus is connected to a pregnant woman's body, then it is part of the woman's body.

5. Any activity that poses a risk to the health of bystanders violates their rights.

6. If two people aren't compatible, then they can't live together.

7. No person should pay taxes to support parts of government that that person doesn't use.

8. If abortion continues to be legal, then respect for life will decline.

9. If Asian and European countries continue to score much higher on international science and math exams, then the United States should adopt their educational methods.

10. All material that arouses lewd desires is pornographic.

11. Any practice that could help cure disease without causing harm should be continued.

12. If gay marriage is allowed in any form, then family life in America will be threatened.

Sample Appraisals: Examples of Techniques of Criticism

As we have learned in the previous sections, an argument can be criticized by (1) showing that the conclusion doesn't follow or (2) showing that one or more premises should not be accepted as true. It is best to determine first whether the conclusion follows. In the process of making this determination, you will typically try adding one or more implicit premises to make the conclusion follow. Having done this, you will have a complete list of the premises you can challenge as you move to the second criticism. If it turns out that there is no plausible way of making the argument valid, then you need not waste your time evaluating the premises, since the faulty pattern will make the argument unsound even if the premises are true. This sequence of criticism is illustrated in the sample appraisal of the arguments in Examples 4.11 and 4.12, as well as in some additional comments on the relation between the two types of criticisms.

Example 4.11

(1) John has withheld information.

(2) Withholding information is lying.

(3) Anyone who has lied has done something wrong.

∴ *John has done something wrong.*

Example 4.12

(1) It is wrong for any person to kill another person.

(2) If the state executes a murderer, then the state is killing a person.

∴ *It is wrong for the state to execute a murderer.*

The initial question concerning either argument, then, is whether the conclusion follows from the premises. Even though the argument in Example 4.11 doesn't exactly fit one of our seven patterns, we can see fairly readily that it is valid. The first two premises—*John withheld information* and *Withholding information is lying*—amount to the claim that John has lied. If we add this to premise 3, we have an argument of the same type as pattern (vi) or Predicate Instantiation, in our list:

(1) All P_1's are P_2's.

(2) m is a P_1.

∴ *m is a P_2.*

That is,

(1) All who have lied have done something wrong.

(2) John has lied.

∴ *John has done something wrong.*

So the conclusion does follow. To admit this is not to admit that the premises are true; but if they are true, then the conclusion must be true as well.

But in the second argument (Example 4.12), there is no such relation between premises and conclusion. Even if it is wrong for any person to kill another person, and granting that the state, by executing a murderer, is killing a person, it doesn't follow that it is wrong for the state to execute a murderer because the state is not a person. There may be special considerations that justify killing by the state. So the second argument can be criticized as invalid.

The second kind of criticism (casting doubt on premises) can be raised against either argument. But before we discuss specific criticisms of premises, we should make some general points about the relation between the two kinds of criticisms. First, as we can see in Example 4.11, if the conclusion of an argument follows, then the only means of criticism left is an attack on the premises. If you decide that there are adequate grounds for believing the premises, then you should be compelled by these reasons to believe the conclusion. If it is impossible for the premises to be true and the conclusion false, and you believe the premises, then it is irrational not to believe the conclusion. Second, if an argument is invalid, then it is not necessary to criticize the premises. You can point out that it does not matter whether the premises are true or not—even if they are true, the conclusion still does not follow.

There is a fairly obvious move, however, that might be made in defense of an argument that has been called invalid: this is to claim that there are implicit premises that, if added, will make the argument valid. In the case of Example 4.12,

Example 4.12
Repeated

(1) It is wrong for any person to kill another person.

(2) If the state executes a murderer, then the state is killing a person.

∴ *It is wrong for the state to execute a murderer.*

it might be claimed that the argument should be expanded by the addition of an implicit premise.

Example 4.12
with Implicit
Premise Added
(implicit)

(1) It is wrong for any person to kill another person.

(2) If the state executes a murderer, then the state is killing a person.

(3) Everything that is wrong for a person to do is wrong for the state to do.

∴ *It is wrong for the state to execute a murderer.*

Your criticism will be more effective if you show that you are aware that the conclusion of an argument can be made to follow by adding premises. (This point was made in chapter 3.) Often the premise or premises left unstated are precisely the ones that, if made explicit, can be seen to be doubtful. A good procedure, then, is to point out first that the argument, as stated, is invalid. Second, you can raise the possibility of adding premises yourself. You might formulate the premise or premises that would make the argument valid, then discuss whether these premises are deserving of belief. In our expanded version of Example 4.12, the added premise says that *Everything that is wrong for a person to do is wrong for the state to do.* To cast doubt on this premise, you can point out that if it were true, then not only would the state be wrong in executing murderers, the state would also be wrong in imprisoning *any* offenders, levying taxes, or generally carrying out any of the functions of government that are beyond the just power of any individual citizen.

We can now return to criticizing the premises in Example 4.11. They were:

1. *John has withheld information.*

2. *Withholding information is lying.*

3. *Anyone who has lied has done something wrong.*

Premise 3 can be criticized by giving counterexamples to this generalization. It is doubtful that someone who has lied to prevent great harm to another has done something wrong.

Premise 2 asserts a conceptual relationship between withholding information and lying. We discuss the criticism of claims such as these at some length in chapter 7. The arguer in this case is guilty of stipulating a meaning of *lying* that is not ordinarily assumed by people who use this word, then proceeding in the argument with this misleading definition.

Premise 1 is the kind of claim that might be criticized on the basis of direct observation or reports of direct observation. Suppose John has been accused of selling his house without telling the buyer that the basement walls leak. Maybe you or someone else actually heard John say that the basement walls leak. Or, in the absence of such direct evidence, the premise could be supported by a further argument that we would then have to evaluate. For example, the buyer of the house could argue that all the junk John piled up against the water-stained wall was a deliberate attempt to hide its condition.

Even if there is direct observational evidence, this doesn't settle the matter with absolute certainty. We sometimes make mistakes about what we see and hear. And studies of "eyewitness testimony" in connection with criminal justice research have clearly indicated that our memory for what we have supposedly seen can be notoriously inaccurate.

Philosophers and logicians have been trying at least from the time of Descartes (1596–1650) to establish unassailable foundations for all our reasoning. Unfortunately, efforts by philosophers to find a list of unassailably true premises with the same kind of certainty and precision that logicians have achieved in establishing the validity of argument patterns have been unproductive if not misguided. Still, we are sometimes justified in *accepting* premises as true, even if we lack absolute certainty. If the arguments in which these premises occur also follow correct patterns (that is, are valid), then we are justified in accepting these arguments as *sound*.

One of the main points of this chapter, which we have tried to emphasize in the sample appraisals we have just considered, is that we have to evaluate two separate features in arguments. We must be aware of each and not get confused.

First there is the structure or pattern—the way the premises and conclusion fit together. When the argument has a correct pattern, we say that *the conclusion follows from the premises,* or to use the more technical term of the logician, the argument is *valid.* Second, there is the content of the premises—broadly, what they say about the world. When we evaluate the premises we decide whether to accept them as *true.* When an argument satisfies both these criteria—when it is *valid* and *all the premises are true*—then it is a *sound argument.* We are then justified in accepting its conclusion.

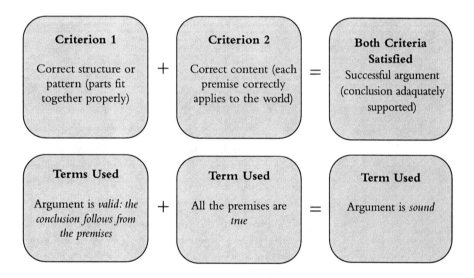

Exercise 4.3   **Distinguishing the Validity of an Argument (That Is, Whether the Conclusion Follows) from the Truth of Its Premises**

---

1. For each argument state

   (i) whether or not the conclusion follows, and if so

   (ii) whether or not the premises are true.

   a. *(1) Every U.S. president has been a faithful husband.*

   (2) Franklin Roosevelt was a U.S. president.

   ∴ *Franklin Roosevelt was a faithful husband.*

b. *(1) Every U.S. president is a U.S. citizen.*

   (2) I am not the U.S. president.

   ∴ *I am not a U.S. citizen.*

c. *(1) If I pay my taxes on time, the Internal Revenue Service will be satisfied.*

   (2) I won't pay my taxes on time.

   ∴ *The IRS won't be satisfied.*

d. *(1) All dogs are mammals.*

   (2) All mammals are animals.

   ∴ *All dogs are animals.*

2. Write in standard form an example (of your own creation) of each of the following:

   a. An argument that is valid but obviously unsound.
   b. An argument that is obviously sound, given common knowledge.
   c. An argument that is invalid and has at least one false premise.
   d. An argument that is invalid but has true premises and a true conclusion.

3. One aspect of the terminology we have introduced may be confusing. In ordinary speech, we occasionally refer to individual statements as "valid," as in "The speaker made a valid point." In these cases, *valid* means "acceptable" or "true." As we are using the term, however, it is only *arguments* that are valid or invalid. Validity does not apply to individual statements. Likewise, only arguments are sound or unsound. On the other hand, only individual *statements* are true or false. It is inappropriate to call an argument true or false.

3(i). Which of the following statements make sensible use of the terms?

   a. The argument you just gave is true.
   b. Your premises are unsound.
   c. Your conclusion is false.
   d. Your statement is true.
   e. Your statement is invalid.
   f. You are arguing from true premises to an invalid conclusion.

3(ii). Which of these statements are consistent—that is, for which of them can the two parts both be true together?

   a. Your argument is sound, but not valid.
   b. Your argument is valid, but your conclusion is false.

    c. Your argument is valid, but not sound.

    d. Your argument is sound, but your conclusion is false.

Some Special Cases: Arguments That We Should or Should Not Do Something

Think of how frequently our discussions focus on whether we should or should not do something. Should we ban smoking in public places? Should potential parents be informed of the gender of their baby-to-be? Should guns be more tightly restricted? Should capital punishment be abolished? These are typical of the issues discussed in newspaper editorials and public forums. Conversations among individuals focus more commonly on personal issues, but even then, the question is often what someone should do.

Because this question is so common, reconstructions of arguments will often take the form of premises that give reasons for or against doing something and a conclusion stating what we should or should not do. We discuss here how these arguments can be treated as roughly fitting certain common patterns from our list, but with certain qualifications.

We Shouldn't Do A, Because A Will Result in B   Consider a reconstruction of an argument from the editorial on gun control that appeared in chapter 3:

Example 4.13
(implicit)

(1) If gun ownership is restricted, then it is easier for criminals to prey on decent folks.

(2) It should not be easier for criminals to prey on decent folks.

∴ Gun ownership should not be restricted.

You will see this general kind of argument again and again.

Example 4.14

A Pattern in Example 4.13[6]

(1) If A, then B.

(2) B shouldn't happen.

∴ A shouldn't happen (or alternatively, we shouldn't do A).

---

6. The "pattern" is roughly stated for simplicity. A closer approximation would be: If A, then B, it shouldn't be brought about that B. Therefore, it shouldn't be brought about that A. If premise A stands for a statement such as "gun ownership is restricted," in the conclusion, Not A stands for something like "that gun ownership is restricted shouldn't happen" or "we shouldn't bring it about that gun ownership is restricted."

Because this kind of argument is so common, it is important to decide whether it can be taken as following a valid pattern. In particular, should we take it as following something like *modus tollens:*

Example 4.15   **Modus Tollens Pattern**

(1) If A, then B.

(2) Not B.

∴ Not A.

The argument pattern in Example 4.14 is similar to *modus tollens* in some respects (but not all). Like *modus tollens,* the pattern of the argument above can be contrasted to a kind of argument that is clearly *not* valid:

Example 4.16   **Invalid Pattern**   **Fallacy of Affirming the Consequent**

(1) If A, then B.   *(1) If A, then B.*

(2) B should happen.   *(2) B.*

∴ A should happen.   *∴   A.*

The conclusion doesn't follow, because (for one thing) there could be other, better ways to make B happen. Consider the similarity between the following two instances of these invalid patterns:

Example 4.17   **Invalid Pattern**   **Fallacy of Affirming
                                                       the Consequent**

*(1) If we restrict the highway speed
     limit to 5 mph, then we would
     reduce highway deaths.*   *(1) If you're a dog, then you
                                                            have feet.*

(2) We should reduce highway deaths.   *(2) You have feet.*

*∴ We should restrict the
   speed limit to 5 mph.*   *∴ You're a dog.*

The conclusions don't follow because there are other, more convenient ways to save lives, and you could have feet by virtue of being something other than a dog.

Although there is a similarity in contrast between these invalid patterns and the patterns in question, there are also differences between *modus tollens* and the pattern in Example 4.13. Both begin by saying that if A happens, then B happens; however, *modus tollens* proceeds to say that B *doesn't* happen, not that it *shouldn't.* Given the premises of *modus tollens,* the conclusion has to follow. Suppose it's really true that *If I study, then I learn,* and that *I haven't learned.*

It follows necessarily that *I must not have studied*. Compare this to the argument that *If gun ownership is restricted, then it will be easier for criminals to prey on decent folks*, and *It shouldn't be easier for criminals to prey on decent folks*. Does it follow with the same kind of necessity that *Gun ownership shouldn't be restricted?*

The answer to this question depends on how we interpret *shouldn't* in the second premise. If it merely means that making it easier for criminals to prey on decent folks is *undesirable*, then the conclusion that we should leave gun ownership unrestricted doesn't follow.[7] One undesirable thing can be outweighed by something else that is more undesirable. The increase in criminals preying on decent folks could be slight, but the increase in accidental deaths due to lack of restriction on firearms could be great. We could then accept that it is undesirable to make it easier for criminals to prey on decent folks, but still conclude that we should restrict gun ownership.

We could, however, interpret *shouldn't* to mean something stronger, such as, "All things considered, this must not be allowed to happen." If it were true in this sense that it *shouldn't* be easier for criminals to prey on decent folks, and true also that restricting gun ownership would have this result, then the conclusion would follow that we should leave gun ownership unrestricted. Keep in mind, though, that this stronger version of the premise would be much more difficult to accept. You would need to consider *all* the likely consequences of restricting gun ownership and of not restricting it, and then decide that the likely increase in criminals preying on the innocent would be an overriding consideration.

The lesson to be learned from the analysis of this kind of argument is to be cautious. If the argument is simply *If A, then B, B is bad, so we shouldn't do A*, then the conclusion doesn't follow. If the argument is taken in the stronger sense of *If A, then B, all things considered B must not be allowed to happen*, therefore *we shouldn't do A;* the conclusion follows but the second premise will be harder to accept.

A slight variation of this same kind of argument is: If we *don't* do A, then B. B shouldn't happen. Therefore, we *should* do A. An instance would be: If we don't restrict gun ownership, then homicide rates will increase. Homicide rates shouldn't increase, therefore we should restrict gun ownership. This argument also is valid only if the second premise is taken in the strong sense, not the weak sense of "it would be undesirable for homicide rates to increase." Again, we must be cautious about accepting this kind of argument.

We Should Do A, Because A Will Result in B   Another kind of argument urges us to do something, not to avoid some unacceptable result but to bring about something good. For example, we should enact the health bill

---

7. Or, if it did follow that we should not restrict gun ownership, it would be only in the weak sense that restricting gun ownership would have one undesirable effect, leaving open the possibility that we should restrict it nevertheless. Surely this is not what the arguer intends.

because more people will receive care. How should we interpret an argument of this kind?

One way *not* to interpret it is by adding an implicit premise to produce the following:

Example 4.18

Faulty Interpretation

(1) If we enact the health bill, then more people will receive care.

(implicit)

(2) More people should receive care.

∴ *We should enact the health bill.*

This interpretation commits the same fallacy as the argument about saving lives by restricting the speed limit (Example 4.17). What, then, is the alternative? We could interpret it along the lines of *modus ponens:*

Example 4.19
(implicit)

Better Interpretation

(1) The health bill will provide care to more people.

(2) If the health bill will provide care to more people, then we should enact it.

∴ *We should enact the health bill.*

Alternatively, we could make the implicit premise more general:

Example 4.20

Alternative Interpretation

(1) The health bill will provide care to more people.

(implicit)

(2) Any bill that will provide care to more people should be enacted.

∴ *The health bill should be enacted.*

It should be noted that premise 1 of either argument might appear in the passage you are interpreting as an if-then sentence *(If the health bill is enacted, then it will provide care to more people).* Such a premise must be rewritten as a simple declarative sentence to avoid making the implicit premise too complicated. (Consider how difficult it would be to understand the following premise: *If it is the case that if the health bill is enacted, it will provide care to more people; then it should be enacted.)*

Arguments like those in Examples 4.19 and 4.20 must also be evaluated with caution. The fact that an action will have *one* good result won't always justify carrying it out. The positive result of extending coverage must be weighed against possible negative results (such as expense in the case of the proposed health bills). Exercise set 4.4 at the end of this chapter includes a number of arguments with conclusions that we should or should not do something. Keep the discussion from this section in mind as you reconstruct and evaluate them.

The Rationale for Using These Critical Techniques

The procedure we have recommended for understanding and criticizing arguments is fairly simple: boil a passage down to its stated premises and conclusion (rephrasing if necessary); add any unstated premises or conclusion; determine whether the conclusion follows and whether the premises should be accepted.[8] Now we raise the question: Why use this procedure? We can give a partial answer at this time by contrasting our procedure to what is probably the most common way of criticizing an argument: simply to attack the conclusion. This approach is in line with the activity of mere disagreement that we contrasted to critical reasoning in chapter 1. The problem with this approach is that it does not help us in progressing toward a better-justified set of beliefs.

The point of interpreting your opponent's position as an *argument* is that then you can make progress toward determining whether one of you should change your position. You can ask whether the reasons (premises) given for the conclusion are ones that you have grounds for believing, or grounds for doubting. And you can ask if the conclusion follows from these reasons (premises).

Let us illustrate this point. Suppose someone has claimed that killing is wrong and capital punishment is killing, so capital punishment is wrong. The least fruitful way of replying would be: "No, capital punishment is not wrong." To stubbornly adhere to this, without regard for the argument that has been presented, is to miss the point of argument and criticism. You have been given reasons for believing that capital punishment is wrong. If you agree with the statements given as reasons, and if the conclusion follows from these reasons, then you should change your mind and agree to the conclusion. If you can show that your opponent should *not* believe the statements given as reasons, or that the conclusion does *not* follow, then your opponent should give up this argument. You could then press your opponent: "Was this the only reason you had for believing your conclusion? Let's look at any other arguments you might have made. Let's look at some arguments against believing that capital punishment is wrong. Perhaps there is an argument on one side or the other that we find conclusive."

Admittedly, there are cases in which it would be appropriate to deny the conclusion of someone's argument. Suppose that someone is presenting an argument that it will not rain today because of the combination of barometric pressure, temperature, and humidity. Just as the person is finishing the argument, you look out the window and see the rain coming down. Of course, it is perfectly appropriate to say, "I don't know where your argument went wrong, but we can see that your conclusion is false."

---

8. An elaboration of this procedure will be presented in chapter 11.

Still, this is an exceptional case. Usually, we make an argument when our conclusion is one that someone might doubt and we do not have a direct means of determining if it is true. That is why we must look for premises to support our conclusion. And in this standard sort of case, it is not appropriate simply to deny the conclusion.

The same considerations apply when you are defending your own position. It is not enough merely to assert unsupported statements. You should build your argument on the firm foundation of true premises interconnected in a valid argument form.

Exercise 4.4   **Criticizing Arguments**

---

1. Write a paragraph or two criticizing each of the following arguments. First, set out the argument. (You might find it useful to sketch a version of the argument in standard form on a piece of scratch paper to help you determine its structure and whether it has any missing premises.) Second, indicate whether the conclusion follows. Third, see if you can cast doubt on any of the premises. (When you do this, don't just make a general statement aimed at discrediting several premises at once; instead, tackle the premises specifically, one at a time, clearly saying which premise you are attacking.) Fourth, consider relevant reformations and whether they can be criticized.

   a. Football should be discouraged, for the reason that football makes people aggressive, and any activity that makes people aggressive should be discouraged.

   b. The United States is not really democratic, since if it were democratic, each person's opinion would have a significant effect on government.

   c. If the government's antidrug policies are effective, then drug use will begin to decline. Drug use is beginning to decline. So the government's antidrug policies are effective.

   d. If you should not be blamed for what your ancestors did, then neither can you take pride in their deeds. It would follow that you are not entitled to take pride in what your ancestors accomplished.

   e. If the average couple has more than two children, the population will rise drastically. But we should prevent the population from rising drastically. So we should prevent any couple from having more than two children.

   f. If the universe was created, then there was a time at which it did not exist. If there was a time at which it did not exist, then there was a time at which nothing was converted into something. But this is impossible. So the universe was not created.

   g. We shouldn't allow doctors to determine the gender of a fetus whenever parents request it. This is so because if we allow such testing, then some parents will abort a fetus simply because of its gender.

     h. People have the right to do whatever they want to with their own bodies. Therefore, a pregnant woman has the right to have the fetus aborted if she wants to.

     i. All tax increases are unjustified at this time. But since user fees to get into national parks are not taxes, increasing them is justified.

     j. No one should get married. This is so because getting married involves promising to live with a person for the rest of one's life. But no one can safely predict that he or she will remain compatible with some other person for life.

     k. People should pay taxes to support only parts of government they use. It stands to reason that people without children shouldn't be required to pay for schools.

2. Read the following newspaper column and reconstruct what you take to be its main argument. (This is to some degree a matter of interpretation.) Write out the argument in standard form so that it follows a valid pattern. Then write a few paragraphs evaluating the premises.

Networks Don't Get Connection[9]
by Cal Thomas

ABC Television broadcast a special "Men, Sex and Rape," last week that was, as *New York Times* reviewer Walter Goodman noted, full of "pretension to virtue."

After the obligatory tabloid-television approach featuring "swelling breasts and buttocks, mostly amid the sands of Palm Beach," as Goodman summarized it, the program attempted to move to the brain for some serious discussion of a troubling subject. The approach had the moral impact of going to confession after a long-planned orgy.

First Amendment absolutists have resisted every attempt to control the huge levels of effluent that have turned our society into a toxic waste dump. Then they create programs like the one broadcast on ABC in which they wring their hands and decry what they have helped to create. It would be like the tobacco industry criticizing the growing number of lung-cancer deaths.

Women are being raped in record numbers—as many as 1,871 per day if one rape-victims rights group is accurate.

One does not have to be a social scientist to see a connection between increased incidents of rape, and other acts of violence against women, and the way women are treated in the popular media. One quick look at MTV offers a sample of the diet on which many young people feed at an early age.

A new Michael Jackson video called "In the Closet" features Michael and a woman thrusting their pelvises at each other. Michael sings, "there's something about you, baby, that makes me want to give it to you."

This video is followed immediately by another called "Baby's Got Back," in which women are shaking their behinds at the camera, various fruits and vegetables shaped like body parts are shown, and the rapper says he likes women's buttocks and feels like "sticking it" to them.

Pornography is worse, of course, but this stuff is what might be called the beginners' material for the raping of the young American mind.

Andrea Dworkin, the feminist writer who has crusaded for tougher anti-pornography laws, wrote a profound letter to the *New York Times* last week in which she told of her own sexual abuse. She believes rape is linked to the tolerance and promotion of pornography and sexual images that give

---

9. Op-Ed, *Seattle Post-Intelligencer,* 14 May 1992, A1. © 1992, Los Angeles Times Syndicate. Reprinted with permission.

cultural permission for men to treat women as objects, not fellow human beings.

To the purists who will not tolerate any controls on "speech" or pictures, Dworkin wrote: "Freedom looks different when you are the one it is being practiced on. Those sexy expletives are the hate words he uses on you while he is using you." Dworkin added that men "act out pornography. They have acted it out on me." She correctly indicted men who hide behind the First Amendment so they can traffic for profit in women's misery. "They eroticize inequality in a way that materially promotes rape, battery, maiming and bondage; they make a product they know dehumanizes, degrades and exploits women; they hurt women to make the pornography, and then consumers use the pornography in assaults both verbal and physical."

For networks (or movie and magazine publishers) to claim that there is no connection, or that they are not responsible if there is a connection, between pictures and words and the brutalizing of women is a lie. Do they tell their advertisers there is no connection between consumer behavior and images of soap, cars and beer? Not if they want to sell ad space and commercial time. For advertisers, they make the opposite claim.

Chris O'Sullivan, a social psychologist who is writing a book on group sexual assault on college campuses, sees a link between sex crimes and visual images. In a letter to the *New York Times,* he wrote: "There is a higher level of aggression, sexual and nonsexual, among those who most often expose themselves to depictions of sexual and nonsexual violence than among those who do not."

Were such a connection established, or even likely, in any other field, government would quickly move to do something about it. Kentucky Republican Sen. Mitch McConnell is trying to take a small step towards clearing up the mainstream of some of this filth in his bill that would compensate victims of sexual assault who could link the assault to pornography. Most of the media establishment has written editorials and lobbied against the bill.

Yet, it is a bill and an idea deserving of support. Women deserve as much protection against rape as it is possible for society to offer. As Dworkin wrote: "A photograph sells rape and torture for profit. In defending pornography, as if it were speech, liberals defend the new slavers. The only fiction in pornography is the smile on the woman's face."

If rape is a terrible crime, and it is, and if there is a connection between pornography and the cultural permission it gives those already predisposed to perform these acts on women, then the government has an obligation and duty to control its proliferation. The McConnell bill is a good place to start.